TAX SAVING
FOR YOUR
BUSINESS

TAX SAVING
FOR YOUR
BUSINESS

**A complete question·and·answer guide to tax
planning for new and expanding businesses**

1987-88

Coopers
&Lybrand

KOGAN
PAGE

The first six editions published in 1981, 1982, 1983, 1984 and 1986 as 'Tax Saving for the Family Business' by
Harrap Limited, 19–23 Ludgate Hill, London EC4M 7PD

This edition published in Great Britain in 1987 by
Kogan Page Limited
120 Pentonville Road, London N1 9JN
by arrangement with Coopers & Lybrand.

British Library Cataloguing in Publication Data

Tax saving for your business.—7th ed.
  1. Tax planning—Great Britain 2. Family
  corporations—Taxation—Great Britain
  I. Coopers & Lybrand (*Firm*) II. Tax
  savings for the family business
  336.2'06   KD5370

  ISBN 1–85091–445–1
  ISBN 1–85091–446–X Pbk

Phototypeset by Input Typesetting Ltd., London SW19 8DR
Printed and bound in Great Britain by Biddles Ltd., Guildford

Contents

Introduction

This book should help anyone running a business, and their employees, to save tax. Saving tax requires compliance with the law and other rules, so the book is also intended to give an understanding of the tax system as it applies to a business.

This is not a full treatise on taxation. It is an introduction to the taxation of businesses and a guide to opportunities for saving tax. After reading this book you should still consult your professional advisors, but you may have some more ideas to discuss with them.

In short compass this book covers a wide range of subjects, as indicated by the chapter headings. For readers who wish to find a topic, there are two ways to use the book. You can refer to a chapter and cast your eye over the questions which introduce each short section. Alternatively you can look up the index which may give several references.

This book is an expanded revision of *Tax Saving for the Family Business*. The present edition takes account of both (pre and post-election) 1987 Finance Acts.

Coopers & Lybrand
Plumtree Court
London EC4A 4HT

August 1987

1
Starting a Business

In what forms can a business be organised?

In the United Kingdom the main forms through which trading
activities are conducted are:

- sole trader
- partnership
- company

There are further possibilities, which are found less often in
practice. These include cooperative organisations normally
registered under the Industrial and Provident Societies Act, the
trustees of a trust, limited partnerships (which must include at
least one general partner fully liable for the firm's obligations),
and unlimited companies, discussed on page 9.

What is the effect of being a sole trader?

A sole trader is an individual who carries on his own trade.
The conduct of business in this way is not regulated by any
specific legislation.

A sole trader's business property is 'his' just as much as his
private property. Equally, he has full responsibility to settle his
debts to his business creditors. This means that it is easy to
start such a trade with minimum formalities, and similarly when
the trade ceases the individual may readily sell the business
property or transfer it to private use. Sometimes property will
be used partly for business and partly for private purposes.

Examples might be a car or even the private residence. In these cases an apportionment of costs will be needed in preparing the accounts of the business.

A sole trader does not have to fulfil any legal requirements in preparing accounts. However, he will need to satisfy the tax authorities, particularly the Inland Revenue as regards the profits of the business, and Customs & Excise if he has to register for VAT. For these purposes he will need to maintain adequate business records and prepare accounts.

What are the main features of a partnership?

Partnership is the relation which subsists between persons carrying on business in common with a view of profit. The Partnership Act 1890, from which this definition is taken, is brief but remains the primary legislation on partnerships. It lays down certain rules for the existence of partnership, and for regulating behaviour between the partners and between them and other parties. The level of regulation is slight compared with that of a company under companies legislation, as described below. Except in Scotland, a partnership is not a separate legal entity apart from the partners themselves.

A partnership can exist between individuals and a company, or may comprise two or more companies. This book considers only partnerships of individuals.

A feature of partnership is that its existence is not always clearly recognised. Whether or not a partnership exists is a question of law based upon the relevant facts. The declaration of partnership is not sufficient to create one but, on the other hand, a partnership can exist without being formally recognised. Except where the position is clearly evident or established in earlier periods, the Inland Revenue may question the existence of a partnership, or the status of an individual as a partner, or may claim that a partnership existed even though it was not recognised. The usual evidence for an individual being a partner is that he or she has a share in the profits or losses of the firm and has authority to bind the firm in its business matters.

What are the main features of a company?

A company is an artificial person created by law. It has a separate legal personality, can sue and be sued, hold property, enter into contracts and carry on a trade or business. Whilst companies can be created for many purposes, most of them are created with objects which are purely commercial, and the powers of a company are usually wholly for the conduct of its trade or business.

Although there is a special form of 'unlimited' company considered further below, the great majority of companies enjoy 'limited liability'. This means that, apart from any personal guarantees, the shareholders are not liable for the company's debts beyond the amount of the share capital which they have undertaken to subscribe.

Separate legal personality and limited liability, probably the outstanding features of a company, may be regarded as privileges by law. Correspondingly, however, there are complex statutory rules regulating the conduct, powers, financial position and accounting and reporting of companies. Most of these rules are nowadays consolidated in the Companies Act 1985 and Insolvency Act 1985. The Companies Act imposes standards for keeping accounting records and requires an annual audit and the filing of audited accounts with the Registrar of Companies.

The separate legal personality of a company brings both advantages and disadvantages, depending on the needs of the business. It means that at the outset the shareholders need to transfer the relevant business or assets to the company. Alternatively, the company is provided with funds for it to acquire the business.

Once the initial stages are passed, however, the corporate structure often has advantages through its separation from the individual shareholders. It means that the ownership of the business is not affected by changes among the shareholders. It also means that there is continuity of management. Furthermore management can be separated from ownership, something which is not possible for an unincorporated business.

The disadvantages of a company arise from its essential feature of being a legal entity separate from its owners:

- The shareholders have rights in the company and, acting together, can control its affairs. Such control does not bring direct ownership of the company's assets, which cannot be applied to the personal benefit of the shareholders or withdrawn from the business at will.

- The administrative requirements under the Companies Acts can be somewhat complex and costly.
- Transfers of shareholdings may be more difficult to organise than changes in a partnership.

What are the tax implications of each form of business?

The sole trader and the partners in a partnership both pay income tax on their trading profits assessable under Schedule D Case I or Case II (see chapter 2). Although a partnership is not a separate business entity except in Scotland, the tax on partnership profits is computed jointly and assessed in the partnership name. The income tax liability of the partnership is the joint liability of all the partners.

Both sole traders and partners are liable to capital gains tax on disposals of business assets. In a partnership disposals are not made by the partnership but are attributed fractionally to each individual partner.

Losses from the trade, like trading profits, accrue directly to the individual and may be offset against other income. During the first four years of a new trade, any losses may be carried back and set against income of the previous three years. Similarly, capital losses are realised by the individual and may offset his other capital gains.

In contrast, a company is taxed as a separate entity. It pays corporation tax (not income tax) on its total profits, including capital gains. Any losses in its trade can be set against its other income and chargeable gains, or against future trading profits. Capital losses can only offset the company's capital gains. In neither case may the losses flow through to cover income or gains of the shareholders.

What are the rates of income tax and corporation tax?

The rates of tax are set by Parliament each year, the income tax year ending 5 April and the 'financial year', for corporation tax, ending 31 March. The tax rates for the year 1987/88 are given in Tables 1.1 and 1.2.

Table 1.1 *Income tax rates for 1987/88*

Taxable income			Rate	Cumulative tax at top of band
(£)		(£)	(%)	(£)
0	–	17,900	27	4,833
17,900	–	20,400	40	5,833
20,400	–	25,400	45	8,083
25,400	–	33,300	50	12,033
33,300	–	41,200	55	16,378
41,200 and over			60	–

The lowest rate (27%) is called the 'basic rate' and applies in many circumstances – for example, on the deduction of income tax at source. The other rates are called higher rates, chargeable on the relevant bands of an individual's total income.

Table 1.2 *Corporation tax rates for 1987/88*

	Rate (%)
Rate of corporation tax	35
Small companies rate	27
Marginal rate (profits between £100,000 and £500,000)	37
Advance corporation tax	27/73

National insurance (NIC) is a major supplementary tax on personal earnings. The rates are given in chapter 6.

Which form is normally best for carrying on a trade?

There is no simple answer, and the best solution depends on the trade and its future prospects. Apart from the factors already considered, the following may be relevant:

- Some professional activities are required by law or professional rules to be carried on by a sole practitioner or by individual partners. This applies to most legal and public accounting services and to certain other professions, although these rules are tending to become more flexible.
- Some businesses are required by law to be carried on normally by a company. This applies particularly to industries where both disclosure and regulation are important features, examples being insurance and banking.

- Sometimes the absence of public disclosure and privacy in financial matters are important considerations. In this case it will normally be advisable to avoid incorporation, unless the use of an unlimited company is proposed.
- If it is likely or intended that the business should have a stock market quotation and offer its shares or securities to the public, it will be necessary for the business to be in a company. An unincorporated business is necessarily private and cannot attract public investment.
- Obtaining limited liability may in some cases be the crucial reason for using a company. This may appear detrimental to creditors, but in reality in many sectors of business other parties including customers and even suppliers and lenders will often be more ready to deal with a company especially for major transactions. The reasons for this include the protection given to creditors by the Companies Act, with statutory audit and filing of accounts, as well as the legal permanence which is attributed to a company.
- In many cases one or more of the commercial factors set out above will determine whether or not a company is used. In other cases some kind of cost/benefit analysis of the company structure should be made. This will take account of the extra administrative costs of a company, together with the comparative tax burden on the business if it is carried on unincorporated or in a company.

Which form saves most tax?

Essentially, this depends on whether the business intends to retain profits for financing expansion or instead will pay out the profits to the individual proprietors.

If profits are to be retained, the rates of tax on business profits beyond modest levels are much lower for corporation tax than for income tax. At £41,200 profits, the rate of income tax reaches 60% but the rate of corporation tax remains at 27% for profits up to £100,000. Of course, company profits would be taxed again if distributed to the shareholders, but in a growing business a proportion of profits will need to be retained to finance expansion so that the only tax they suffer is corporation tax.

On the other hand, if the profits are to be distributed to the proprietors, there will normally be a saving of tax by carrying on the business outside a company, so avoiding payment of Class 1 NIC (see chapter 6).

It is difficult to set out general rules covering every business, but an example may help. Let us assume that a business has profits for the year to 31 March 1988 of £60,000 and the proprietor (single, and with no other income or deductions) needs £15,000 after tax to live on. The tax payable with the business in a company or carried on by a sole trader is as given in Table 1.3.

In the following example, there are tax savings through incorporation, owing to a significant proportion of profits being taxed only at the small companies rate of corporation tax (27%). If instead the shareholder had drawn out most of the profits in remuneration, the company structure would have been more costly in tax. A comparison along these lines should be made for every new business.

Table 1.3 *Example comparing tax paid by company and sole trader*

(a) Using a company

	(£)	(£)	Total tax and NIC (£)
Company		60,000.00	
Profits before salary			
Salary (see below)	21,806.00		
NIC (employer)	2,278.72		2,278.72
		24,084.72	
		35,915.28	
Corporation tax (27%)		9,697.12	9,697.12
Profit retained in company		26,218.16	
Individual		21,806.00	
Salary			
Income tax	5,425.40		5,425.40
NIC (employee)	1,380.60		1,380.60
		6,806,00	
		15,000.00	
Total profit available to company and individual		41,218.16	
Total tax and NIC paid			18,781.84

Table 1.3 *continued*

(b) Individual as a sole trader

	(£)	(£)	(£)	Total tax and NIC (£)
Profits			60,000.00	
NIC: Class 2		204.05		
Class 4		677.25		
		881.30	881.30	881.30
Income tax				
Profits		60,000,000		
Less: ½ Class 4 NIC	339.00			
Personal allowance	2,425.00			
		2,764.00		
		57,236.00		
Tax on first	41,200.00	16,378.00		
Tax on	16,036.00	9,621.60		
	57,236.00		25,999.60	25,999.60
Total profit available to individual			33,119.10	
Total tax and NIC paid				26,880.90

Saving of total tax and NIC through company (£26,880.90 − £18,781.84) = £8,099.06.

Do I get any tax relief in starting a business?

There are certain reliefs designed either to permit the offset of trading losses against other income or to reduce the risk of loss from investment in a trade:

- A sole trader or partner can claim to offset losses (including capital allowances) arising in the first four tax years in which a trade is carried on against any income in the three tax years before the loss arose, taking the earlier year first. (Alternatively, under normal rules for loss relief an individual trader may set a loss against other income of the tax year in which the loss is made or the following tax year.)
- For companies, the Business Expansion Scheme (BES, see chapter 5) allows an outside minority investor to deduct the amount of investment in shares up to £40,000 per year against taxable income.

- An individual who subscribes for new shares in an unlisted UK trading company is given a choice if subsequently he makes a capital loss on disposal of the shares. If preferred, instead of setting the loss against capital gains, he can set it against other income of that or the following tax year.

Since BES relief is not available to substantial shareholders or to employees, it is evident that the direct offset of losses is only available for the individual trader or partner. However, the right to offset capital losses on shares subscribed in an unquoted trading company is not restricted to outside shareholders and may reduce the risk of investment for the managers of such a company.

Is there any advantage in using an unlimited company?

There are three advantages in using an unlimited company:

- No capital duty is payable on amounts subscribed for shares in an unlimited company.
- An unlimited company may purchase or redeem its share capital without restrictions imposed by the Companies Acts. The tax position, however, is the same as for a limited company.
- An unlimited company does not have to file accounts with its annual return to the Registrar of Companies. A number of companies, including some very well-known concerns, have been formed as or re-registered as unlimited companies for this reason.

The disadvantage of unlimited liability means that a shareholder on the register at the time of liquidation and former shareholders who sold or transferred their shares within one year previously, may be called upon to meet any liabilities of the company that are not satisfied out of the proceeds of realisation of its assets. There is no question, however, of a member (or a former member) having to meet the company's liabilities whilst it remains a going concern.

2

Tax on Trading Profits

How are businesses charged to tax?

Any business, whether it is carried on by a sole trader, partnership or company, is chargeable to tax on its total profits including capital gains. A sole trader and, likewise, the individuals who make up a partnership, pays income tax on his income and capital gains tax (CGT) on his capital gains. Companies, on the other hand, pay corporation tax on their total profits, that is the total of income and capital gains.

From its beginnings the UK system of tax on income has retained the structure of distinguishing different kinds of income according to their origin or 'source'. It is sometimes known as the 'schedular' system, because each kind of income is assessed under a 'schedule' and some schedules are subdivided into 'cases'.

In principle there are separate rules for computing and assessing income under each schedule and case, although in practice some of the rules are very similar. The schedules and cases are set out on the following page.

The accounts of a business may include income from a number of these sources, but for most businesses the primary source is Schedule D Case I (profits of a trade). An individual carrying on a profession is taxed under Schedule D Case II, for which the rules are generally identical with those of Case I. A company's profits of a trading nature are always charged under Schedule D Case I and not Case II.

Schedule A: rents and other income from land (including buildings) in the UK

Schedule B: income of any occupier of woodlands managed upon a commercial basis

Schedule C: income from government securities (tax deducted at source)

Schedule D:

Case I	profits of a trade
Case II	profits of a profession or vocation
Case III	interest, annuities and annual payments
Case IV	income from foreign securities
Case V	income from foreign possessions (including shares and land)
Case VI	income not falling under any other schedule or case

Schedule E: emoluments from an office or employment (charged under three cases) pensions and social security benefits

Schedule F: dividends from companies resident in the UK

Will I be taxed on the trading profits shown in my accounts?

It is very seldom that the trading profits for Case I purposes are the same as the accounts profits, and the Inland Revenue will rarely accept the accounts profit figure without further analysis, for the following reason. The profit or loss in a trader's accounts for a normal year will be a net figure of trade receipts, usually sales, less expenses including the cost of goods sold, depreciation, employment costs, premises and overheads, finance costs and accounting adjustments such as provisions against stocks and debtors. The tax rules, described below, will usually require adjustments to the accounts in computing the taxable profit, and there will often be some non-trading items which should be analysed under the correct schedule and case.

The courts have held consistently that the taxable profits of a trade must derive from a profit and loss account prepared on 'the ordinary principles of commercial accounting'. There is no legal requirement for an individual (sole trader or partner) to prepare accounts of his trade, although a company is required to publish audited accounts. The Revenue insist on obtaining these audited accounts from all companies but their main requirement from all taxpayers is for a detailed profit and loss account. A balance sheet is also required to identify items which do not feature in the profit and loss account such as capital spending and certain reserve movements, but the main emphasis is on the profit and loss account.

If my trading accounts need adjustment for tax purposes, do clear rules exist to show the adjustments needed?

Nowhere are the rules clearly set out, because the relevant law is based on tax cases as well as statute. Some of the main rules, a little simplified, are as follows.

Statutory rules

1 Capital expenditure may not be deducted. This includes not only the cost of capital assets and their depreciation, but also professional costs of acquiring or improving a capital asset. (However, capital allowances may be allowed on such expenditure.)
2 Expenditure not for the purposes of the trade (e.g. excessive remuneration of family members, fines) is not allowed.
3 Business entertaining is not allowed, except for entertainment of staff and overseas customers.
4 Any costs of private or family expenditure are disallowed.
5 The cost of improving property is not allowed, and the cost of repairs is not allowed until expenditure is incurred.
6 Tax is chargeable on 'the full amount of the profits or gains' of the period. This means that the Revenue will often refuse to accept a swings-and-roundabouts approach as to the year in which profits arise.
7 UK company dividends are not taxed in the hands of another company, but are of course taxable in the hands of any individual.
8 Interest on overdue tax is disallowed and similarly 'repayment supplement' on late repayments of tax is exempt from tax.

Some rules of case law

9 The 'profits' of a trader chargeable to tax are the profits for the relevant period prepared according to the ordinary principles of commercial accounting, with such adjustments as tax law requires.
10 The accounts of a trader must include opening and closing values of stock-in-trade. Stock may be valued at cost or net

realisable value if lower. Apart from the rule for valuing stock, no provision may be made for a future loss.

11 An expense may be deductible even though there is not yet a liability to pay, but costs not yet incurred cannot be charged. An example of the first is a warranty provision on goods sold and of the second a provision for costs of a future reorganisation.

12 Expenses covering a specific period of time (e.g. rent, rates, leasing charges, wages and salaries) are deductible in proportion to the duration of the accounting period, and not according to the invoice date or the time of payment. (This is an example of the fundamental accruals concept of accounting.)

13 Just as a trader's expenditure is not always deductible as an expense, so not all receipts are trade receipts, for example:

- government grants toward capital expenditure either offset the capital expenditure or, in the case of Regional Development Grants, are ignored for tax purposes;
- sales proceeds of a capital asset or part of the business are charged under capital gains rules;
- if a lump sum ('reverse premium') is received by a lessee on entering into a lease, this may not be chargeable;
- in rare cases a trader may receive a sum which is really a gift, in that it does not arise from commercial dealings;
- payments on account or in advance will usually not be trading revenues of the period of receipt, although they will become income as the work is completed.

What are capital allowances and what are the current rates?

While the cost of capital assets and related depreciation is disallowed, the legislation allows a form of depreciation for tax purposes known as 'capital allowances'. The intention is to restrict allowances to certain favoured assets and to impose standard rates of write off. For the year 1987/88 the main rates of capital allowances are as given in Table 2.1.

Not every kind of capital expenditure has equivalent capital allowances, and the exclusions include expenditure on financial investments, goodwill, land, office buildings, shops and related premises such as banks and non-industrial warehouses, and most payments for leases.

Table 2.1 *Main classes of capital allowances*

		Writing-down allowances (%)
New and second-hand machinery or plant or commercial vehicles	(a)	25
New and second-hand motor cars (in most cases)	(a)	25 (max. £2,000 per car per annum)
Industrial buildings purchased new in the period	(b)(c)	4
New buildings and fixed plant therein in enterprise zones		100
Qualifying hotels	(b)(c)	4
Agricultural buildings and works	(c)	4
Patent rights and 'know-how'	(d)	25
Mining works and oil wells	(d)	25
Mineral deposits and rights	(d)	10
Scientific research (excluding land or dwellings)		100

(a) These allowances are on the reducing balance basis and may be disclaimed wholly or in part.
(b) The above allowances apply to expenditure on construction (new buildings and alterations). Special rules apply to expenditure on used buildings.
(c) These allowances are on the straight line basis.
(d) These allowances are on the reducing balance basis.

At the rate of 25% on the reducing balance, plant is written off over roughly nine years. For items which are in fact retained for less than four or five years, a claim may be made to treat them as 'short-life assets' (see below).

What are the definitions of 'machinery or plant' and 'industrial buildings'?

There is no statutory definition of the term 'machinery or plant'. Machinery is generally recognisable but 'plant' has a wider meaning. The courts have consistently upheld a century-old case definition of plant as being 'whatever apparatus is used for permanent employment in the business.' The crucial insight here is that 'plant' does not have a static definition as a range of assets, but the 'plant' for each trade depends on the nature of the trade concerned. For example, a swimming pool was held to be plant of a seaside caravan park, law books were plant of a barrister and interior lighting and decor have been accepted as plant for a hotel.

Industrial buildings allowances, as they are known, are available for expenditure on an 'industrial building or structure'. The term 'structure' may include such matters as bridges, roads or car parks.

There is a statutory definition of an industrial building or structure, expressed in relation to the activities of the trade where it is employed. These activities include not only the familiar manufacturing, but also trades of transport, water, power generation, mining, agriculture and certain forms of storage. Whatever the trade, certain kinds of buildings are excluded and these include houses, shops and offices. The legislation has been extended to cover certain qualifying hotels.

What are 'enterprise zones'?

Enterprise zones are areas designated by the Government which, for a period of ten years, enjoy special incentives for economic development. Some of these incentives are local (such as nil or reduced rates and simplified planning controls). The main incentive as regards Inland Revenue taxation is that expenditure on the construction of all commercial buildings (including offices and shops) qualifies for industrial buildings allowances, at a rate of 100% in the year of expenditure.

Enterprise zones are all relatively small in area, and are typically sited in regions of economic blight or dereliction which are felt to require special incentives for outside investment.

How are the allowances for machinery or plant worked out?

Items of machinery or plant including furniture, fixtures and fittings used for the business qualify for a 25% 'writing down' allowance on the reducing balance, so that equipment costing £16,000 will be eligible for £4,000 capital allowance in the first year, £3,000 in the second, £2,250 in the third and so on. In effect this means that the expenditure is written off for tax purposes after about nine years. In practice all such assets are combined into one large 'pool' of expenditure. A similar allowance is available on motor cars, except that the allowance on cars costing over £8,000 is restricted to £2,000 per year.

What happens when I sell the assets?

The proceeds of disposal, up to a maximum of original cost, are deducted from the existing pool of expenditure, so that the taxpayer will have allowances equal to his net cost (i.e. cost less proceeds). In the case of a building or expensive car there is no such 'pool' so that the proceeds are deducted from the residue of expenditure and the net difference is either a 'balancing charge' or a 'balancing allowance'. For buildings constructed since November 1962, allowances and adjustments such as balancing charges cease to be made more than twenty five years after the building was first used.

A building or other asset qualifying for capital allowances remains within the capital gains rules, and a sale for more than original cost may give rise to a capital gain.

Do I get capital allowances if I lease rather than buy outright?

Under most leases the ownership of the asset remains with the lessor, who thereby has entitlement to the capital allowances. There can be significant tax benefits in leasing if the taxpayer is making losses because the lessor will use the allowances and may share the benefit with the lessee by way of reduced lease rentals.

Under a hire purchase (or 'lease purchase') agreement, the hirer has an option to purchase the equipment at the end of the hire period. It is normal accounting practice that such assets are treated as belonging to the hirer. The capital allowance rules similarly treat the asset as if it belonged to the hirer throughout the contract, so that the hirer (and not the existing owner) can claim allowances on the full capital cost once the asset has been brought into use for the hirer's trade.

When can I claim capital allowances?

Capital allowances can be claimed for the accounting period in which the expenditure is 'incurred' which is the date when the obligation to pay becomes unconditional. This will normally be the date when title to the asset passes which is usually also the date taken for accounting purposes in recording the purchase of the asset. If the terms of the purchase provide that the period between incurring the expenditure and paying the liability exceed four months, the relevant date becomes instead the due date of payment.

In some circumstances it may be worthwhile postponing a claim to capital allowances, for instance if the company is making losses or the individual or partner would not otherwise use his personal allowances in full. This is done by making a formal 'disclaimer' of allowances. By this means, unwanted allowances are avoided and the expenditure on which allowances are computed in future periods is increased.

You say assets are effectively written off after nine years, but some of my plant is scrapped much sooner – can I get quicker relief?

The 'pool' of expenditure into which all plant falls means that capital allowances may continue to be claimed long after the asset has been scrapped. In view of this the taxpayer can elect to treat most assets (but not motor cars and certain other assets) that have a useful life of five years or less as short-life assets for which allowances are computed separately. When the assets are sold, the net cost can then be claimed in full.

Example

A computer is purchased in 1987 for £20,480 and sold for £2,000 in 1990; accounts are drawn up for calendar years.

	No election Cost or Residue	Allowances	Short-life asset election Cost or Residue	Allowances
	(£)	(£)	(£)	(£)
1987	20,480	5,120	20,480	5,120
1988	15,360	3,840	15,360	3,840
1989	11,520	2,880	11,520	2,880
1990	8,640		8,640	
less: proceeds	(2,000)		(2,000)	
	6,640	1,660	6,640	6,640
1991	4,980	1,245		
1992	3,735	etc.		

With the short-life asset election all the allowances of £18,480 (£20,480 − £2,000) have been claimed by the year of disposal.

What was stock relief and is it still relevant?

Stock relief, which was abolished in 1984, was an allowance designed to offset the unrealised gains reported in accounts which were due to inflation increasing the value of stocks. Some businesses may have tax losses forward created in part by stock relief which may be subject to restriction if not used within six years of the relief being claimed.

Will my business be liable to capital gains tax?

Capital gains tax is charged on the disposal of chargeable assets. A chargeable asset is any asset, subject to a few exemptions, on which a profit would not be treated as income. The gain is the excess of net sale proceeds over their original cost, as adjusted for the increase in inflation since purchase (or March 1982 if later). This adjustment is called the 'indexation allowance' and is normally based on cost but an election can be made for the indexation allowance to be based on the market value of the asset at 31 March 1982, the date the allowance was introduced. (See also page 119.)

Example

A owns a freehold shop which he acquires in 1976 for £8,000. He sells the premises for £40,000 in March 1987. The value of the shop in March 1982 is estimated to have been £26,000.

A would elect for market value at March 1982 to be used as the basis for indexation. The Retail Price Index increased 26.6% between March 1982 and 1987.

	(£)
Sale proceeds	40,000
Less: cost	8,000
	32,000
Less: indexation allowance: £26,000 × 26.6%	6,916
Capital gain	25,084

A could then use his exempt allowance for 1986/87 of £6,300 to leave a chargeable gain of £18,758.

Individuals and partners are liable to the tax at 30% and companies are liable at their rate of corporation tax. Most asset sales will be liable to capital gains tax including land, buildings, goodwill, plant and shares, although motor cars are exempt.

A form of relief from capital gains tax called 'rollover relief' is available to most types of business. Capital profits on the sale of assets used for the trade can be 'rolled over' and set against the cost of certain assets purchased between one year before and three years after the sale, so long as that asset is also used in the trade. This period can be extended at the discretion of the Inland Revenue. This effectively means that if proceeds are continually reinvested then any capital gains tax liability can be continually deferred. Sales of assets not used in the trade such as shares do not qualify for rollover relief and will always be liable to capital gains tax.

Rollover relief is available on sales and purchases of any of the following assets, and it is not necessary for the purchase and sale to be of the same type of asset:

- Buildings or land occupied (as well as used) only for the purposes of the trade.
- Fixed plant or fixed machinery.
- Ships, aircraft and hovercraft.
- Satellites and spacecraft.
- Goodwill.

For an individual this relief can extend across more than one trade so that the gain on the sale of a shop (which may include gains on fittings, building and goodwill) can be rolled over against the acquisition of for instance a hotel. For companies which form part of a 75% group (see page 41) gains in one company can be rolled over against purchases in another. A gain will however crystallise to the extent that the proceeds are not re-invested.

Example

A in the previous example re-invests the proceeds in a new freehold shop costing: (a) £50,000; (b) £37,000; (c) £12,000.

	(a) (£)	(b) (£)	(c) (£)
Proceeds not re-invested	–	3,000	28,000
Capital gain crystallising	NIL	3,000	25,084
Base 'cost' for capital gains tax purposes of new shop: cost	50,000	37,000	12,000
Less: gain rolled over	(25,084)	(22,084)	–
Deemed cost for CGT	24,916	14,916	12,000

If the new asset is a depreciating asset (that is, it has a useful life of less than 60 years, such as a short lease or fixed plant) the gain is 'held over' up to ten years. During that time the deferred gain may be matched with further expenditure on a non-depreciating asset.

3

Tax Planning for Sole Traders and Partners

How is my tax liability calculated?

An individual is liable to tax on all sources of income including taxable business profits after deducting allowances and reliefs. Income tax is charged on a graduated scale, rising from a basic rate of 27% to a highest rate of 60% (see page 5).

In the case of an employee earnings are taxed under Schedule E and tax is generally deducted by the employer on a weekly or monthly basis via the Pay As You Earn ('PAYE') system with any necessary adjustments being made on an annual basis once all the relevant information is to hand.

Self-employed individuals are taxed under Schedule D Case I or II on the profits of their business, but there is no equivalent of the PAYE system. In the case of a sole trader all the profits are obviously assessable on him. In the case of a partnership, the tax liability of each partner is calculated on his or her share of partnership taxable profits, together with any other non-partnership income. The tax liability on his share of partnership profits is, however, assessed and charged on the partnership and is a liability of the firm. It is therefore usually advisable for a partnership to retain sufficient funds to meet its tax liabilities before paying out its profits to the individual partners.

For what period are profits charged to tax?

Income tax is assessed for the year ended 5 April. The taxable profits of a person carrying on a trade either alone or in partnership (but not a company – see chapter 4) are normally assessed to income tax on a basis called the 'prior year basis'. This means that the assessment for any tax year will be based on the profits of the accounting period ended in the previous tax year. Thus, for a trader or partnership which prepares accounts to 30 September, the assessable profits for the 1988/89 tax year will be the taxable profits of the accounts for the year ended 30 September 1987 (i.e. the accounts year ended in the 1987/88 tax year).

When a business starts, this prior year basis clearly cannot be applied and there are special rules governing the calculation of assessable profits for the first three tax years of trading. In the first tax year the actual profits are assessed to tax. In the second tax year the profits of the first 12 months of trading will normally be assessed. In the third tax year the assessable profits will generally be either:

- the profits of the first 12 months once again, or;
- if there is a complete accounts period of 12 months ended in the second tax year, that period of 12 months, or;
- exceptionally, the profits of the 12 month period ended on the accounting date in the previous fiscal year.

An example best illustrates how this works:

Mr X started in business on 1 January 1987 and prepared accounts for a 21 month period to 30 September 1988 producing taxable profits (that is after adding back disallowable items such as depreciation and entertaining and deducting tax allowable items) of £31,500. He selected 30 September as his regular accounting date. His profits adjusted for tax purposes for the year to 30 September 1989 were £10,000.

Table 3.1 *Profits assessed on the basis of the first 12 months' trading*

Tax year	Basis	Basis period	Calculation	Assessment (£)
1986/87	Actual	1. 1.87– 5. 4.87	31,500 × 3/21	4,500
1987/88	First 12 months	1. 1.87–31.12.87	31,500 × 12/21	18,000
1988/89	First 12 months	1. 1.87–31.12.87	31,500 × 12/21	18,000
1989/90	12 months ended 30.9.88	1.10.87–30. 9.88	31,500 × 12/21	18,000
Total profits assessed				58,500

These rules can work to the disadvantage of the taxpayer, particularly if proportionately larger profits are earned in an early period of trading which is then used up to three times (as above) to ascertain the profits charged to tax in the first three years. However, the taxpayer may elect to have the profits of the second and third tax years assessed on an actual basis. In the example above, the result of this election would be as shown in Table 3.2.

Table 3.2 *Profits assessed on an actual basis for the first three years*

Tax year	Basis	Basis period	Calculation	Assessment (£)
1986/87	Actual	1. 1.87– 5.4.87	31,500 × 3/21	4,500
1987/88	Actual	6. 4.87– 5.4.88	31,500 × 12/21	18,000
1988/89	Actual	6. 4.88– 5.4.89	(31,500 × 6/21 + 10,000 × 6/12)	14,000
1989/90	12 months ended 30.9.88	1.10.87–30.9.88	31,500 × 12/21	18,000
Total profits assessed				54,500

In certain circumstances even further savings can be obtained by planning the length of the first accounting period. If, in the example above, the first accounts were for the nine months to 30 September 1987, showing tax profits of £6,300, and the second set of accounts, showing tax profits of £25,200, were for the year to 30 September 1988, the assessable profits would be as shown in Table 3.3.

Table 3.3 *Profits assessed with a planned length of first accounting period*

Tax year	Basis	Basis period	Calculation	Assessment (£)
1986/87	Actual	1.1.87– 5. 4.87	6,300 × 3/9	2,100
1987/88	First 12 months	1.1.87–31.12.87	6,300 + (25,200 × 3/12)	12,600
1988/89	First 12 months	1.1.87–31.12.87	6,300 + (25,200 × 3/12)	12,600
1989/90	Prior year	Year ended 30.9.88		25,200
Total profits assessed				52,500

When a business ceases there are again special rules to calculate the assessable profits in the last three years of trading. In the final tax year the actual profits are assessed to tax. The Inland Revenue also has an option to assess the previous two tax years taken together on an actual basis (rather than on a prior year basis) if this gives rise to higher assessable profits. Further special rules are also required when there is a change of accounting date.

As if all this were not complicated enough, there are then also different rules for allocating capital allowances in both opening and closing years. In each case, the general effect of these rules is to prevent capital allowances being claimed more than once.

Can I use these rules to my own advantage?

The effect of all these special rules is that certain profits are charged to tax more than once (and in some cases three times) whilst some profits can escape tax altogether. It is therefore advantageous where practicable to incur allowable expenditure in those periods which are taxed more than once. Equally any additional income should, if possible, be earned in the period which escapes tax.

Unfortunately it is not always possible to influence the timing of income and expenditure of a new business in this way. It is, however, often possible to select the optimum combination of choice of accounting date and length of initial accounting period. As shown in the example above an incorrect decision at this early stage can lead to a significantly higher overall tax liability being incurred on the same level of profits. Good professional advice is essential if exposure to these additional liabilities is to be avoided.

The option to elect for the actual basis of assessment to apply in the second and third years of assessment must also be carefully considered, particularly if profits are fluctuating. As a general rule the option for the actual basis would not be beneficial if tax profits are rising. Each case should, however, be considered individually.

The choice of cessation date is also important since it will determine which tax years' profits can be adjusted by the Inland Revenue. Again, an example best illustrates this:

Mr. X, who has traded successfully for a number of years

decides to retire at the end of March 1988. His adjusted profits are as follows:

	(£)
Year ended 30 September 1984	20,000
Year ended 30 September 1985	20,000
Year ended 30 September 1986	28,000
Year ended 30 September 1987	33,000

His profits from 1 October 1987 onwards are £2,000 per month.

The Inland Revenue will almost certainly decide to exercise their option to assess the two tax years prior to cessation on an actual basis. This is because the rising profit trend will mean that taxable profits will be higher on an actual basis than on the prior year basis. The assessable profits would therefore be:

Tax year	Basis	Calculation	Assessment (£)
1985/86	Actual	(½ × 20,000) + (½ × 28,000)	24,000
1986/87	Actual	(½ × 28,000) + (½ × 33,000)	30,500
1987/88	Actual	(½ × 33,000) + (6 × 2,000)	28,500
			83,000

By continuing to trade for one further month Mr. X would of course generate a further £2,000 of profit. He would also have a cessation in 1988/89 rather than 1987/88 and would save some tax, since the total assessable profits for the years 1985/86 to 1987/88 would then be:

Tax year	Basis	Calculation	Assessment (£)
1985/86	Prior year	Year to 30 September 1984	20,000
1986/87	Actual	As above	30,500
1987/88	Actual	As above	28,500
			79,000

The assessment for the tax year 1988/89 would be £2,000.

What happens if a sole trader takes on a partner or if a partner joins or leaves the partnership?

When there is a change in partners, or a sole trader becomes a partnership, there is a 'cessation' of the old partnership and a 'commencement' of a new partnership for tax purposes. However if at least one partner continues in the business (even as a sole trader) the old and new partners can elect that it be treated as continuing. If the election is made the partnership continues to be taxed on the prior year basis as though no change had taken place.

If an election could be made to treat the partnership as continuing, but is not made, the normal cessation rules apply to the old partnership. The assessments on the new partnership are calculated in a similar way to a new business, that is on actual profits for the year of change, but in the case of a partnership the actual basis continues for the three following years of assessment. In the fifth year the business will return to the prior year basis, subject to the partners' right to elect for taxation on actual profits in the fifth and sixth years.

There are certain circumstances where a cessation can be beneficial and other circumstances where a cessation would give rise to substantial additional tax. If the continuation basis is to be adopted a formal election must be submitted to the Inland Revenue within two years of the date of change. This date is obviously long before the partnership will know for certain whether or not such an election is beneficial, but if the level of profits for the third year is reasonably predictable it is usually possible to make the correct decision within the two year period.

When do I have to pay the tax?

Income tax on business profits is normally payable in two equal instalments, on 1 January in the year of assessment and on the following 1 July, as are Class 4 national insurance contributions which must be paid by the self-employed individual or partner.

As an example of this, consider a trader (or partnership) who prepares accounts to 30 September and has been trading for a number of years. The profits for the year ended 30 September 1987 will be assessable to tax in the fiscal year 1988/89 and the income tax and Class 4 national insurance contributions will be payable in equal instalments on 1 January 1989 and 1 July 1989.

Interest on overdue tax may be charged by the Inland Revenue in certain circumstances where tax is paid late.

Owing to the 'prior year' basis the choice of accounting date will determine the time span between when profits are earned and when tax is payable. To obtain the maximum deferment from the time profits are earned until they are assessed to tax an advantage may lie (depending on the trend of profits) in having an accounting date early in the fiscal year (which starts on 6 April). This can be seen from the following example.

Period of accounts	Tax year in which the accounts end (the 'prior year')	Tax year in which profits are assessed	First payment due
Year to 30 June 1987	1987/88	1988/89	1.1.89
Year to 31 March 1987	1986/87	1987/88	1.1.88

As the opening years rules show, income tax is payable by a business every year. In the above example the long period between the accounting date (30 June 1987) and the due date for the first instalment of tax computed on that year (1 January 1989) does not signify a full deferral of tax for that time. What is deferred is payment of tax on any increases in profits and if profits fall there is similar delay in having a lower tax charge.

What happens if I make a loss?

A tax loss may be set against any other income of the taxpayer for the tax year in which the loss is made, or against income of the following tax year, or both.

Example

A trader has been trading for a number of years and prepares accounts to 30 June. The accounts for the year ended 30 June 1987 show an adjusted profit for tax purposes of £10,000 but because of substantial capital expenditure the claim for capital allowances based on the accounts is £18,000. A tax loss of £8,000 therefore arises. For the purpose of loss relief, it is treated as arising in the tax year in which the loss-making accounts period ends – i.e. in 1987/88. The loss is available for relief against any other income for the tax year 1987/88 and/or 1988/89. In addition, because a loss has been created, there would be a nil business income tax assessment raised for the fiscal year for which the accounts form the basis period (i.e. 1988/89 in this example).

In electing to set the loss against other income it is important to try to ensure that personal allowances are still utilized. If in the example above other income totalled £8,000 and personal allowances £3,000, the effect of a loss relief claim for £8,000 would be that no income would be chargeable to tax. The personal allowances of £3,000 would therefore be wasted.

It is not possible to make a claim only in respect of, for instance, £5,000 of the loss but it may be advantageous not to claim certain of the capital allowances in that year so as to reduce the loss for the year to the appropriate amount.

In the example above the effect of disclaiming £3,000 of writing-down allowances at 25% (see page 15) would be as follows:

	(£)	(£)
Other income		8,000
Less: Loss relief –		
Original loss	8,000	
Less disclaimed allowances	3,000	
		(£5,000)
Total income		3,000
Less: Personal allowance		(3,000)
Taxable income		Nil

The £3,000 disclaimed allowances would then be available in later years. If the average tax rate in those years was, say, 50% the effect of that disclaimer would be to save £1,500.

The claim for loss relief would normally be against the total income of both the taxpayer and his or her spouse. The claim can however be restricted to the taxpayer only if this is beneficial (for instance because personal allowances are available to cover the spouse's income).

During the first four tax years in which the trade is carried on, a claim can also be made to set losses against any of the taxpayer's income in the three tax years before the loss arose, taking the earliest year first. This rule can help to cover some of the financial risk in starting a new trading venture because it means that at the start of a business, when losses are often made, tax can be recovered from earlier years, thus assisting cash flow.

If no claim is made under either of these available reliefs, the losses are carried forward and may be set only against future profits of the same trade.

Relief is also available for losses incurred on the cessation of a trade. Losses sustained in the 12 months before the date of discontinuance, so far as not otherwise relieved as above, may be carried back and set against profits of the trade for the three tax years prior to that in which cessation occurs, taking the latest year first.

In order to claim any loss relief the taxpayer must show that he or she was carrying on the trade on a commercial basis with a view to profit. This will exclude certain hobby businesses but most traders will meet the test. There are also special rules which restrict the relief for losses from farming and market gardening where a loss has been incurred in each of the previous five years.

Is tax relief given on expenditure incurred prior to commencement of trading?

As a general rule tax relief is given on expenditure incurred prior to the commencement of trading provided that the expenditure would have been allowable if incurred after the trade had commenced. There are however separate rules for capital and revenue expenditure:

- for capital allowance purposes money already spent on capital assets is deemed to be incurred at the start of trading and the normal allowances are given in the opening period;
- allowable revenue expenditure incurred up to three years before trading starts is treated as a loss sustained in the opening year of assessment.

Will it save tax if I employ members of my family?

Savings in tax can be made by paying a wage or salary to other members of your family particularly if they have otherwise unutilized personal or other allowances to set against that income. Depending on the level of profits an overall saving may also arise because a higher proportion of 'profits' are charged at the basic rate of tax rather than at the higher tax rates. However, any salary or wage paid must be commercially justifiable and must be incurred wholly and exclusively for the purposes of the trade (see page 12). Employing members of your family may also give rise to additional liabilities for national insurance contributions. It will therefore usually be advisable to check the calculations carefully beforehand.

Will it save tax if I introduce members of the family as partners?

Savings in tax can be made by sharing business profits among a number of partners who will each benefit from the lower bands of income tax. For tax purposes as in general law a partner is one of two or more individuals carrying on a business in common with a view to profit. A partner is necessarily someone who can commit the partnership and shares in its management. If some members of the family do not participate in this way the Inland Revenue will probably not accept that they are partners for tax purposes. Subject to these factors husband and wife may be business partners and they may then elect for separate taxation of the wife's earnings. This election can reduce the total tax bill in certain cases where total income is fairly substantial and both husband and wife have earned income.

The introduction of a new partner into a business (whether a member of the family or some other person) means that the business is deemed to cease for tax purposes and to recommence unless all persons engaged as partners in the business both before and after the change elect that the business should be treated as continuing. The effect of a cessation and recommencement is briefly described on pages 22–24.

What pension arrangements can I make?

A self employed person qualifies for the basic state pension only and not the earnings related pension. It is usually advisable to secure a further pension by paying additional contributions. The rules are currently undergoing some change and are discussed in detail in chapter 10.

What happens if I sell my business?

For income tax purposes the trade is deemed to have ceased on the date of sale of the business and the cessation rules (page 23) will apply. In this connection the date of cessation will be a crucial factor in minimising the effect of any closing years adjustment by the Inland Revenue.

The disposal of the business may also give rise to a capital gains tax liability on those business assets which have a value in excess of cost plus indexation. One asset frequently overlooked in this connection, perhaps because it is often not included within the formal business accounts, is goodwill. The excess of the price paid for the business over the market value of its net assets will be treated as a payment for goodwill and be subject to capital gains tax in the normal way, unless retirement relief (page 34) or rollover relief (page 19) may be claimed.

It will generally be necessary to apportion the total price paid for the business between, for instance, stock in trade, plant and machinery, property and goodwill. If the amounts received in respect of plant and machinery (or industrial buildings) exceed their written down value for tax purposes they may give rise to a balancing charge for capital allowances (see page 17) and possibly therefore to a higher income tax liability. To the extent that the proceeds received are in excess of the original cost of the asset, they are however taken into account only for capital gains tax purposes and do not give rise to a balancing charge. Since the rates of income tax and capital gains tax may be different (the rate of income tax potentially being 60%) the allocation of the purchase price between the various assets may have a significant effect on the overall tax liability. The allocation of the purchase price must of course be commercially justifiable but some flexibility usually exists within this constraint.

Can I transfer my business into a limited company?

As a business grows it is often advantageous for a number of reasons to operate the business through a limited company (see chapter 4). Unfortunately the transfer of an existing business into a limited company brings about a number of unavoidable tax consequences:

- The trade carried on by the individual or partnership is deemed to have ceased for income tax purposes on the date of the transfer. The cessation rules therefore apply (page 23). The profits in the final tax year will be assessed on an actual basis and the Inland Revenue has the right to assess the two previous tax years on an actual basis rather than on a prior year basis. If profit levels are stable then this is of little consequence. If, however, profits are rising steadily the effect is to create a liability to tax which would otherwise have been either deferred or avoided completely.

- Stamp transfer duty at 1% (or in the case of shares and securities at ½%) of market value will be payable on assets transferred to the company, other than those which can pass by physical delivery. There is an exemption for transactions not exceeding £30,000 in value but this does not extend to shares and securities. The charge will normally exclude stocks and most machinery, but will cover land, buildings and fixtures, goodwill, debtors and investments. No stamp duty will be payable on the debtors however if they are collected by the owners of the old business rather than assigned.
- Capital duty will be payable at 1% on the value of the net assets contributed to the company in exchange for the company's shares.

The transfer of the business also gives rise to a disposal for capital gains tax purposes. It is however possible to defer the capital gains tax liability by using one of two available reliefs.

The whole of the capital gains tax liability is deferred provided all the assets of the business (or all the assets of the business other than cash) are transferred to the company and provided that the whole of the transfer price is settled by the issue of shares in the company to the sole trader or partners. Capital gains tax is then payable only when the shares themselves are sold, at which time additional reliefs such as retirement relief (see below) may well be available to minimise the overall liability.

The requirement to issue shares in respect of the whole of the transfer value does however mean that profits from previous years which have been retained within the business can no longer be withdrawn without incurring additional tax liabilities. Since it will frequently be necessary to withdraw funds in order to pay income tax liabilities for periods prior to the transfer, the issue of shares effectively means that a double charge to tax will arise.

It may be possible to minimise this double charge by extracting surplus profits from the business prior to incorporation; this would also save capital duty. Care must however be taken if it is clear that the withdrawn funds will have to be reintroduced to the company as loans shortly after the transfer.

If an exchange wholly for shares is likely to create problems of this nature (or indeed if the proprietors simply wish to retain some flexibility as to the subsequent withdrawal of funds from the company) it may be possible in certain instances for those business assets with an inherent chargeable gain to be transferred to the company either at original cost or, in the case of goodwill, at a nominal value. In this case the inherent gains are then chargeable on the company only when the assets in question are subsequently disposed of. If this route is available there is no need to issue further shares to the proprietors of the business. There are a number of potential pitfalls in this route and careful planning is essential.

Can I operate a company alongside my business?

It is possible to operate a company alongside an existing business but care must be taken to ensure that the company does not effectively carry on the trade of the business. If this is the case then the Inland Revenue may argue that the trade of the business has been transferred to the company and may seek to apply the special cessation rules (see page 23). The effect of applying these rules could then be to give rise to higher income tax liabilities in the two tax years prior to the year in which the transfer is deemed to have taken place.

In certain circumstances it is nevertheless possible, with careful planning, to use a company operating in parallel to enable a successful and growing business to plan the timing of its incorporation so as to avoid, or at least minimise, the effect of the special cessation rules. New opportunities for an existing business frequently offer scope for such planning but there are dangers for the unwary.

Is there any relief from capital gains tax when I retire?

If you are over 60 (or retire because of ill health) and either sell or gift the whole or part of a business which you have owned for a qualifying period of 10 years you are exempted from capital gains tax on the first £125,000 of any gains arising in respect of the 'chargeable businesss assets' of the business. The amount of relief is reduced proportionately if the full 10 year qualifying period is not met. 'Chargeable business assets' will generally include assets used for the trade of the business (except those specifically exempt from capital gains tax such as motor cars) and will certainly include goodwill. Investments, or assets held as investments rather than for the purpose of the trade, will however not qualify for retirement relief and capital gains tax on such assets must be paid in the normal way.

The relief also covers the disposal of shares in a trading company which has been your 'family company' provided that you have been a full time working director of the company over the qualifying period. A 'family company' is one in which you have at least 25% of the voting rights or in which you have at least 5% personally and you and your immediate family together have more than 50% of the voting rights. In the case of a disposal of shares in a family company only the proportion of the gain which relates to 'chargeable business assets' qualifies for relief.

You do not need actually to retire in order to obtain the relief provided you are aged 60 or over. The relief is also available to both husband and wife individually provided they both meet the qualifying conditions. For a long established business owned jointly by husband and wife the total relief could therefore amount to as much as £250,000. Clearly the introduction of a wife as either a partner or fellow shareholder and director will need to be planned up to ten years in advance in order to take full advantage of retirement relief.

4
Tax Planning for Companies

Is corporation tax separate from income tax and capital gains tax?

Yes. Companies are liable to corporation tax on their 'profits', which are defined as income and chargeable gains. Up to 16 March 1987 companies paid an effective rate of 30% on chargeable gains, but the new rule is that all profits are charged at the same rate.

How is corporation tax charged and paid?

The rates of corporation tax are set for each 'financial year' which ends on 31 March (see page 5). Tax is charged on the current year's profits and there is no equivalent of the prior year basis of income tax. The tax is assessed on a company for its accounting periods which are normally the periods for which it prepares accounts. Where the accounting period falls into different financial years the profits are apportioned and charged at the appropriate rates of corporation tax in force in each financial year.

Corporation tax is payable by most companies nine months after the end of the accounting period. A company can choose the date of its year end but the choice will not affect the payment interval for corporation tax.

What is the 'small companies rate'?

A company pays the 'small companies rate' of corporation tax if its profits do not exceed £100,000. For profits between the lower limit of £100,000 and an upper limit of £500,000 (at which the normal rate of corporation tax applies on all profits) there is still relief but it is withdrawn over a band of profits charged at a higher marginal rate. In recent years the small companies rate has been identical to the basic rate of income tax, as shown in Table 4.1.

Table 4.1 *Small companies rate of tax*

Financial year	Period	Corporation tax rate (%)	Small companies rate (%)	Marginal rate (%)
1986	1 April 1986 to 31 March 1987	35	29	36.5
1987	1 April 1987 to 31 March 1988	35	27	37

If a company has 'associated' companies both the lower and upper limits are divided by the total number of associated companies. This can lead to a loss of relief if profits are not evenly spread among associated companies. Equally there is an opportunity for a larger business to claim relief. If one associated company has profits of £1 million and the other has profits of £50,000, the latter company can claim full relief. Despite anomalies such as this, small companies relief is intended to encourage the smaller company by a lower rate of tax.

What happens on payment of a dividend?

A dividend is a payment to shareholders and cannot exceed the company's distributable reserves (profits after tax).

On paying a dividend a company must pay 'advance corporation tax' (ACT) at a rate which is related to the basic rate of income tax. For 1987/88 the basic rate is 27% and the ACT rate is 27/73 so that if a dividend of £73 is paid the ACT will be £27. In the hands of a shareholder the ACT is called a 'tax credit' and is added onto the net dividend to determine the shareholder's gross income. In the above example the shareholder is treated as having gross income of £100 on which tax of £27 has been accounted for. For shareholders paying only basic rate tax, their liability will be entirely satisfied by the tax credit. Where the aggregate dividend takes the taxpayer's total income above the basic rate limit (£17,900 in the year 1987/88) additional tax on the margins above the 27% basic rate will be payable up to the maximum rate of 60%. For example, if a £73 dividend is subject to tax at the maximum rate the additional liability is:

	(£)
Aggregate dividend (£73 + £27)	100
Income tax (60%)	60
Tax credit	(27)
Additional tax payable	33

For many family businesses, the alternative to a dividend is a director's bonus which will attract National Insurance contributions (see chapter 6). In such cases a dividend will be cheaper in overall cost than payment of additional salary.

If dividends are planned, there are further matters to consider:

- Dividends must be paid at the same rate per share on all shares of the same class. Dividends may be waived by individual shareholders, but the tax consequences of a waiver can be complex.
- Paying dividends may increase the value of minority shareholdings.
- The timing of dividends should be planned to ensure prompt recovery of ACT against corporation tax (see below).

Is ACT a cost to the company?

ACT is advance corporation tax, that is a payment in advance of the company's charge to corporation tax. In principle it should not increase the total corporation tax payable. It is always paid earlier than corporation tax and is due within fourteen days of the end of the calendar quarter (or of the accounting period if earlier) in which the dividend is paid.

The amount of corporation tax which can be settled by ACT varies according to the basic rate of tax. In the financial year 1987, the maximum offset is 27% of profits. This will fully settle a liability to tax at the small companies rate, but otherwise leaves a liability of $35 - 27 = 8\%$ to be settled in cash.

If the ACT cannot be used fully because of nil or insufficient profits, the excess (known as 'surplus' ACT) may be set against

corporation tax due for the six years prior to the period of the
dividend. Such a claim will usually lead to a repayment of
corporation tax.

Alternatively, ACT may be 'surrendered' to cover the corporation tax liability of any company which was a subsidiary
throughout the period.

Finally, ACT may be treated as recoverable in the accounts
against tax on profits expected in the following year. If none of
these circumstances is present, the ACT will be written off as
part of the tax charge in the accounts. It will remain as a 'hidden'
asset to reduce future charges to corporation tax. In practice a
dividend should seldom be paid without reasonable certainty
that the ACT will be recoverable.

What is the significance of a 'close company'?

A close company is one which is 'controlled' by five or fewer
'participators' (shareholders, with holdings aggregated with
those of their associates) or by any number of directors. In
practice nearly all family companies are close companies.

The purpose of close company legislation in the past has been
to prevent the avoidance of the higher rates of income tax, by
retaining profits within a company taxed at the lower corporation tax rates, instead of distributing them to the shareholders.
This purpose was achieved by rules which 'apportioned' undis-
tributed profits, that is, treated the shareholders and the
company as if a dividend had been paid.

Under current legislation, there is no apportionment of the
trading income of close companies, so that close company legislation for the most part has ceased to be severe. Companies still
have to distribute their investment income and half their estate
income (for example, rental income received by property investment companies) unless, in the case of trading companies, they
can show a business need to retain it. If dividends are less
than the income which should be distributed, the deficiency
is 'apportioned' to the shareholders. (In this situation the tax
liabilities may be paid by the company.)

If a close company makes loans to participators it must pay
tax at 27/73 of the loan, the current rate of ACT (see also page
37). This tax payment is recoverable when the loan is repaid.
In addition there are special rules to ensure that any benefit
provided to a shareholder is treated as his income.

As a practical matter, the rules described above have little impact upon a close trading company or group, while close company status can bring an important advantage in connection with interest relief. An individual may claim a deduction against income for interest paid on a loan used to acquire shares in or lend money to a close trading company or group (or a qualifying property investment company), provided that he or she has a 'material interest' in the company (more than 5% of the ordinary shares) or holds any part of the ordinary share capital and works full-time in the management of the company. Where individuals are planning to raise funds for investing in a company, it is often vital that the company is close at the outset. If later on the company ceases to be close through shareholder changes, the investors will continue to have relief on existing, but not on subsequent borrowings.

What level of salary should the company pay to the shareholder directors?

Salaries should be set for commercial reasons, but tax factors also need to be considered.

- A company will get a deduction for tax purposes for salaries which are paid wholly and exclusively for the purposes of the trade, and not merely to suit the tax arrangements of the shareholders. Salary levels must, therefore, be justifiable in relation to services performed. In practice many trading companies may be able to justify paying substantial salaries.
- Shareholder directors in an expanding company will often take less than commercial salaries to help the company's finances. Salary levels in future years cannot be justified by reference to salary foregone in the past and if payment of salary is tax effective for the company it is possible for the shareholder to lend back the cash.
- The rates of corporation tax, now only 27% for small companies, may create an incentive to restrict directors' remuneration. Whereas retained profits will only be taxed at 27% in many cases, the individual will pay income tax at rates up to 60% and the company will pay up to a further 10.45% in NIC. The rate of tax payable on part of the salary would then be 43.45% greater than the rate of tax if it had been retained as a profit. The decision on salary levels is then a matter of balance between saving tax and the needs of the

individual for income. Although salaries can be costly in tax, the pension contributions payable for an employee (including a shareholder director) are based on the individual's record of earnings in the employment, and this is a further reason for taking reasonable salaries.

How are losses treated for corporation tax purposes?

A company which incurs a loss in its trade will normally only be able to carry that loss forward to be offset against future profits from the same trade. However, in the period in which the loss arises, the company can elect to offset the loss against any other profit (including capital gains) of the same period, and if there are still losses unrelieved they can be set against any profits of the previous period. This facility for setting trading losses against capital gains of the same or prior period is a feature of corporation tax which has no equivalent in income tax rules. Capital losses can only be offset against current or future capital gains.

Within a group of companies, losses may also be applied for group relief, and this is discussed below.

Is there any way the shareholders can benefit from the company's losses, either directly or by sale of the shares?

There is no direct way of the shareholders obtaining any benefit in the form of relief for the company's loss.

Where a company is sold, giving a change of ownership, there are special rules which can prevent the company's losses being available to cover its future profits. This means that an intending purchaser of a company will be wary of regarding unrelieved tax losses as an 'asset' (although with careful planning they may often be preserved) so that the vendors always have difficulty in obtaining any additional consideration for the loss.

A shareholder who has subscribed for shares in an unquoted trading company may obtain some tax benefit if he or she makes a loss on disposal of those shares (see page 115).

Shareholders of a close trading company or group can relieve it of financing charges by borrowing money themselves and either lending to the company interest free or investing the money in the company's shares. Either way a shareholder holding more than 5% or working full time in the management of the company should obtain relief for the interest paid (see page 39).

How should new activities be organised?

When a business first starts, the activities may not amount to 'trading' for tax purposes, but when trading starts expenses incurred within the previous three years may be deducted. If there is further development expenditure by a trading company, this can usually be written off as a trading expense, but where it is segregated in a new company no deduction is allowed until the new company starts to trade. At worst, if the new activity is a failure so that trading never begins, there will be no tax relief for the expenditure. By contrast, if development activities are conducted in an existing trading company, expenditure will normally be deductible as incurred.

Another strong reason for avoiding too many companies is the effect for loss relief. If there is a trading loss in a period, it can be carried back (see page 40), surrendered for group relief, or carried forward in the company. Where a business is carried on through numerous companies, profits may arise in certain companies while there are losses brought forward in the others. If instead the business is organised in one company, usually it will be treated as one trade for tax purposes, and there will be full offset of losses and profits.

What reliefs are available for a group of companies?

For most tax purposes a 'group' is a parent company and its 75% subsidiaries. Each company is still taxed on an individual basis but in certain important respects they are treated as one business for tax purposes:

- 'Group relief' is available, meaning that profits and losses of a common period may be offset.
- Dividends may be paid to the parent without liability for ACT and interest can be paid gross within the group.
- Capital assets may be passed between group companies without crystallising a chargeable gain.
- ACT may be surrendered to a subsidiary (see page 38).

A 90% grouping also gives relief from stamp duty on transfers of assets within the group.

Can a company purchase its own shares?

Recent legislation allows limited companies, if empowered by their articles, to purchase their own shares subject to certain safeguards. The company must purchase the shares out of profits available for payment of dividends or out of a new issue of shares made for the purpose.

A private company (but not a public company) may buy its shares out of capital (once it has used its distributable profits) but subject to stringent safeguards for the protection of shareholders and creditors. These safeguards include:

- statutory declarations of solvency to be made by the directors (and reported on by the auditors) which must also cover the company's ability to remain a going concern for the following year;
- publication in the *London Gazette* and the national press;
- rights of creditors or dissenting shareholders to object;
- provisions whereby past members and the directors may have to contribute to the assets to the extent of the payment out of capital if the company becomes insolvent.

Unlimited companies may buy or redeem their own shares without restriction (see page 9).

What are the taxation effects?

The general tax rule is that any payment made by the company to its shareholders in the purchase of its own shares will be treated as a distribution (which means that it will be taxed as if it is a dividend), except to the extent that the shareholder is receiving back the amount subscribed for the shares. Recent legislation provides that, in certain circumstances, an unquoted trading company may purchase its own shares without its shareholders being treated as if they had received a dividend. The shareholder, however, must bring the proceeds into his or her capital gains tax computation. This relief applies to:

- payments to shareholders applied towards payment of capital transfer tax or inheritance tax liabilities arising on death and for which they are liable (but only in cases of hardship);

- purchases or redemptions of shares made wholly or mainly to benefit the trade and not designed for the purposes of avoiding tax (see page 117).

There are certain conditions that the shareholder must meet which are that he must be resident and ordinarily resident in the UK and have owned his shares for at least five years, his percentage holding in the company must be reduced by at least 25%, and he must not retain a holding in the company exceeding 30%.

The legislation provides for a procedure whereby the company may obtain advance clearance from the Inland Revenue. In practice it will always be necessary for the company to obtain this clearance.

Can a company pass its business back to the individual shareholders as a going concern?

The transfer of a business into a company is helped by a number of reliefs from tax (see page 32). There are no equivalent reliefs for transferring a business out of a company, and unless the business is small or has incurred losses, heavy tax penalties may arise in the following ways:

- The company would cease trading, balancing charges would arise, and any tax losses would disappear.
- There would be a disposal of assets at market value for chargeable gains purposes.
- In the hands of shareholders the assets received in excess of the original investment would be taxed either as a dividend or as a capital gain.

As described on pages 6–8, a successful business which retains its profits is often best organised through a company to benefit from the lower corporate tax rates. Some smaller businesses may have good reasons for returning from an incorporated to unincorporated structure. The obstacles created by the tax system in the way of such changes are now recognised. Recently a consultative document was issued jointly by the Inland Revenue and the Department of Trade and Industry, with proposals for some relaxation in the tax rules to assist disincorporation by small private trading companies. It now seems quite probable that there will be relieving legislation for this purpose.

5

The Business Expansion Scheme

What is the Business Expansion Scheme?

The Business Expansion Scheme (BES) was introduced in 1983, replacing the Business Start-Up Scheme of 1981. Both schemes were designed to give relief for investment in unquoted companies, but the Business Start-Up Scheme was only available where the trade was new. Shares that qualify under the BES can be issued by existing as well as by new companies, and there is no restriction on the quantity or proportion of shares which can qualify.

Originally the BES legislation was drafted to take effect for four years to 1987, but the Government decided that the scheme was a success in its purpose of enabling smaller companies to raise risk capital, and so the legislation has been made permanent. The essence of the scheme is that individual investors get relief against income tax on monies subscribed for ordinary shares issued by a qualifying trading company or companies, the maximum qualifying subscription being £40,000 for any individual in a tax year. As the required investment is in ordinary shares, it follows that only a company (and not a sole trader or a partnership) can raise money under the scheme.

What companies qualify?

Companies eligible to participate in the scheme must be unquoted companies so that companies listed on the Stock Exchange or dealt in on the Unlisted Securities Market are excluded. Companies can however have their shares quoted on the over-the-counter share market or on the 'third market' organised by the Stock Exchange.

The company must be incorporated and resident for tax purposes in the UK.

The company must carry on a qualifying trade wholly or mainly in the UK or be a holding company of qualifying subsidiaries (being subsidiaries owned at least to the extent of 90% which also trade wholly or mainly in the UK).

Most genuine trades qualify under the scheme if they are conducted on a commercial basis and with a view to realising a profit. Certain trades are specifically excluded and these relate mainly to dealing in commodities, securities, land, goods other than in the course of normal wholesale or retail distribution and most financial, legal and accountancy services. If the value of the interests in land held by the company at any time is more than half the value of the company's assets as a whole, the company ceases to be a qualifying company except that it may issue £50,000 of qualifying shares in a year. This rule was intended to counter the tendency for many issues to be promoted in 'asset-backed' trades such as farming, property development and hotels.

Are there any further restrictions on the company?

There are restrictions relating to both the control of the company and its share capital structure which the company must satisfy for a period of three years from the time it issues its new shares or, if later, commences trading. These are as follows:

- The company must not be a subsidiary of another company.
- The company must not either on its own or together with a person connected with it (see below) control another company which is not a qualifying subsidiary. In addition no arrangement can be in existence at any stage during the three year period whereby either could come about.
- The company must begin trading within two years of the shares being issued (if it is not already trading at that point) otherwise the claim for BES relief will not be allowed.
- All the company's issued shares must be fully paid up. The shares on which investors claim BES relief must be newly issued ordinary shares which during the period of five years from the date of their issue carry no present or future prefer-

ential rights to dividends, to be redeemed or to receive the company's assets on a winding-up. Care must be taken that if any non BES shares can be redeemed such redemption will not lead to withdrawal of relief from BES investors (see below).

Who can invest under the scheme?

In order to qualify, an individual investor must be resident and ordinarily resident in the UK at the time when the shares are issued.

The main restriction is that the individual must not be 'connected' with the company. This rule reflects the underlying policy of the legislation to attract 'outside' investment and not to subsidise the investment of those who are committed to the company either as employees or as major investors. These restrictions apply throughout the period from two years before the share issue until five years afterwards.

- An individual is 'connected' with the company if he is an employee, director or partner of the company. He is also 'connected' if an 'associate' of his is an employee, director or partner of the company. 'Associate' includes a close relative defined as husband or wife, parent or ancestor and children or remoter issue. This means, for example, that an individual cannot get relief for investing in a company of which his grandson is an employee. The only qualification to this rule is that an unpaid director may get relief, and he may do so despite receiving reimbursement of expenses and payment for certain professional services.

An example may illustrate these restrictions:

Mrs X, Mr Y and Miss Z each subscribe £10,000 on 1 July 1987 for 10,000 ordinary shares of £1 each in a qualifying company with a total issued ordinary share capital of £100,000.

Mrs X is a former employee who left the company in 1986.

Mr Y is a non-executive director of the company and only receives reimbursement of expenses incurred.

Miss Z is the daughter of an employee.

Mrs X is connected with the company as she was an employee within two years of making her investment.

Mr Y is not connected with the company so long as he only

receives reimbursement of his expenses and no other remuneration.

Miss Z is connected with the company being the daughter of an employee.

● An individual is also connected with a company if he (or an associate) possesses or may obtain more than 30% of the issued ordinary share capital, voting power or combined loan capital and issued share capital of the company.

An individual may invest through a nominee. From 1986 joint investment is permitted. A husband and wife living together are in effect treated as one for BES purposes and together they can invest up to the individual limit of £40,000 a year.

What are the limits on investment?

The maximum subscription by an individual for eligible shares in any year of assessment is £40,000. In order to qualify, the individual's subscription for shares in any company during the year must be at least £500. This lower limit is not imposed upon investments made by an approved 'investment fund' but the individual is always required to invest at least £2,000 in a subscription to a fund.

Is the scheme not too restrictive and complicated?

Although the legislation is complicated it is possible to implement a simple scheme which will qualify under the BES rules. A company intending to issue shares under the scheme should seek Inland Revenue clearance that its shares will qualify although inevitably such clearance will not take account of future events unforeseen at the time of the share issue. Because BES relief can be withdrawn due to the occurrence of events beyond the investors' control individual investors may require indemnities from the company, its directors and shareholders that such events will not be brought about by their actions.

How do I set about finding investors for my company?

For a private company this is not easy, because by law a private company may not offer its shares to the public. It may be possible for friends (not 'connected' with the company) to invest. Some institutions or stockbrokers may channel private investment.

The BES rules also envisage investment being organised by an 'investment fund' approved by the Inland Revenue. These funds act as intermediaries. The potential investor gives the fund authority to make his investments using its expertise, and usually his investment is spread across several companies. From the company's point of view, as long as its business prospects are appealing, an approach to an investment fund may give the opportunity to raise substantial equity capital without the practical or legal difficulties of a public offer.

Where the funding requirement is large, the company will probably need to become a public company and acting with an institution offer its shares publicly with a full prospectus. BES relief in such cases may enable an issue to be launched which would not be acceptable to investors as a straight equity offer.

When do investors get tax relief?

Relief is given for the tax year in which the shares are issued. If, however, shares are issued before 6 October in a tax year then the investor can elect to have up to £5,000 or 50% of the investment (whichever is less) related back to the preceding tax year subject to the overall limit of £40,000 relief in each tax year. Tax relief must be claimed by the investor within two years from the end of the tax year in which the shares are issued or in appropriate cases within two years from the end of the first four months of trading. The claim cannot be made until the company has traded for four months and must be accompanied by a certificate from the company.

Example

On 1 July 1987 Ventures Limited issues to Mr A 1000 new £1 ordinary shares at a premium of £9 per share for which Mr A pays £10,000. The shares are intended to qualify for relief under the BES and Mr A elects to have £5,000 of his investment related back to tax year 1986/87. Ventures Limited begins its qualifying trade on 1 February 1988.

Mr A is not entitled to claim relief until 1 June 1988 (because relief cannot be claimed until the company has been trading for four months) but the relief of £5,000 will then be given for each tax year 1986/87 and 1987/88. If Mr A had not elected to relate back £5,000 of his investment the relief would have been given wholly in 1987/88. Mr A must make a claim by 31 May 1990.

If Ventures Limited had already been trading for four months on 1 July 1987, it could have sought immediate Revenue clearance that the shares were eligible under BES and issued the necessary certificate to Mr A, who could then have claimed relief. He would need to make the claim by 5 April 1990.

How is tax relief given?

Investors are given tax relief by deducting the amount of their investment from their taxable income. Accordingly tax relief on the investment is obtained at the investor's marginal rates of income tax by way of a repayment of tax paid. Where relief has been given and not withdrawn and the shares have been held for five years there will be no liability to capital gains tax on any subsequent disposal.

Example

The facts are as above. Mr A will receive relief on his investment as follows:

1986/87	(£)
Earnings	18,000
Investment income	12,000
Total income	30,000
Less: Single Person's Allowance	(2,335)
	27,665
Less: BES investment of £5,000 related back	(5,000)
Taxable income	22,665
Income Tax thereon	7,297
Compared with tax payable before BES relief on income of £27,665	9,660
Tax saving on BES investment	2,363

1987/88	£
Earnings	20,000
Investment income	13,000
	33,000
Less: Single Person's Allowance	(2,425)
	30,575
Less: BES investment of £5,000	(5,000)
Taxable income	25,575
Income Tax thereon	8,170
Compared with tax payable before BES relief on income of £30,575	10,670
Tax saving on BES investment	2,500

The net cost of the £10,000 investment, after tax relief of £4,863, is in this case £5,137.

Can tax relief be denied or withdrawn?

There are a number of events affecting the investor or the company which could lead to the withdrawal or denial of relief.

- Relief will be withdrawn in part or in full if the investor disposes of his scheme shares within five years of issue.
- Relief will be denied if the shares are 'replacement capital', that is the investor is one of a group who formerly controlled the trade, and the same group controls the company.
- Relief is denied where an individual is involved in 'parallel trades'. This arises when an investor is one of a group of persons controlling the company and on his own or as one of a group of individuals controls another company which carries on a similar trade to that of the BES company.
- Relief will be reduced by any value received by the investor from the company (which includes any benefit by way of loan or repayment of a loan or salary but not dividends).
- Relief will be withdrawn to the extent that the company repays any of its other share capital.
- Relief could be denied if a company which makes substantial losses thereby infringes the requirement that no more than 50% of its net asset value is attributable to land.
- Relief may be denied unless the shares are subscribed and issued for bona fide commercial purposes and not as part of a scheme to avoid tax.

Can an investor dispose of his shares without losing tax relief?

When an investor has held his shares for five years he may deal freely with them without any loss of relief. BES shares issued after 18 March 1986 are exempt from capital gains tax on their disposal by an individual. Shares issued earlier are within capital gains tax with the cost subscribed deductible from proceeds. A qualifying investment cannot give a capital loss.

Death is not treated as a disposal and any subsequent disposal, even within the five year period, will not result in a withdrawal of tax relief.

What happens if the company is taken over?

Relief is withdrawn, even if there is a share for share exchange which is not a disposal under capital gains tax rules.

Should my company consider the issue of BES shares?

There is no doubt that the BES does involve restrictions for a company, as for its shareholders. Unless these restrictions are readily acceptable, it may be better to avoid small issues of BES shares.

However, for some companies the raising of equity capital under the BES may be the best option for funding. The circumstances will include the need for long term funding, without the prospect for some years of a Stock Exchange quotation. The tax relief may cause investors to subscribe for shares which, as an ordinary equity issue, would be uncompetitive through risk or the uncertainty of future earnings.

Although BES investors may accept high risk, they naturally want an attractive investment. This will include means for selling their shares after five years if desired. A company raising BES capital will need to consider in advance the alternatives, which include purchase of shares by the company, sale to an institution, or a quotation on one of the stock markets.

6

Understanding National Insurance

What are National insurance contributions, and who must contribute?

National insurance contributions (NIC) are really a form of additional income tax on earnings. The funds raised are used in part towards financing the social security benefit system.

Contributions are payable under four classes, according to the status of the individual (provided that he meets certain conditions as to residence or presence in the UK).

Class 1	For directors and employees. Contributions are payable by the individual ('primary contributor') and his employer ('secondary contributor').
Class 2	paid by the self-employed.
Class 3	Voluntary contributions (made for example by people overseas) to maintain qualification to certain benefits, mainly the retirement pension.
Class 4	Paid by the self-employed.

What income is subject to NIC?

NIC is charged on 'earnings' which for this purpose includes remuneration or profit from any trade, business, profession, office or vocation. Not all earnings are subject to NIC – for example, there are various thresholds below which NIC is not payable. Similarly there are 'ceilings' above which NIC is not payable. Also, the term 'earnings' has a special definition which excludes various items from chargeability. A common example of this is that most benefits in kind for employees, such as the benefit from company cars, are not 'earnings' subject to NIC, whereas they are chargeable for income tax.

What are the rates of NIC?

The rates of NIC vary according to the class of contributor and usually apply for the whole of a tax year. The standard rates for 1987/88 are set out in Table 6.1.

Table 6.1 *National insurance contributions for 1987/88*

Class 1 contributions from 6 April 1987 Standard rates on all earnings per week	Equivalent annual earnings up to £	Employee	Employer
if earnings are between:			
Nil and £38.99	2,027.99	NIL	NIL
£39.00 and £64.99	3,379.99	5.00%	5.00%
£65.00 and £99.99	5,199.99	7.00%	7.00%
£100.00 and £149.99	7,799.99	9.00%	9.00%
£150.00 and £295.00	15,340.00	9.00%	10.45%
If earnings exceed £295.00	15,340.00	£26.55	10.45%

Notes

(a) Contributions are normally paid on payments made in the normal pay interval, i.e. a week, month or other pay period. Although directors pay employee rates, the annual limits above apply in most cases and contributions are normally based on pay in the year (see below).

(b) On earnings between £39 and £295 per week (or £2,027.99 to £15,340 per year), lower rates apply if under the company pension scheme employees are 'contracted out' of the earnings-related state pension.

(c) Contributions are payable on cash earnings and on payments made for employees but not on non-cash benefits.

(d) The appropriate percentage in the table applies to all earnings in the pay period and not just that marginal band.

(e) For men over 65 or women over 60 there are no employee contributions but employer contributions are as above.

Class 2 contributions

£3.85 per week
Not payable by a male over 65 or a female over 60.

Class 3 contributions

£3.75 per week.

Class 4 contributions

6.3% on profits, computed broadly as for income tax between £4,590 and £15,340 per annum (maximum £677.25 per annum).
Not payable by a male over 65 or a female over 60.

The table shows that very different rules for NIC apply for employment earnings and profits of the self-employed. For example:

- Total contributions from a company and a director or employee with an annual pay period are 19.45% on earnings which exceed £7,800 and are less than £15,340. On earnings over £15,340 the director or employee pays nothing but the company pays 10.45%.
- Maximum contributions for a self-employed individual or partner are £881.30 in 1987–88 (Class 2 and Class 4 together).

How is NIC accounted for and what records are needed?

In the case of class 1 contributions, it is normally the employer's responsibility to deduct employees' (primary) contributions from their earnings, and to pay employer's (secondary) contributions. This should be done as part of the normal PAYE process with each payroll, including the maintenance of deduction working sheets. The NIC is then paid over to the Inland Revenue with the PAYE, by the 14th day of the following tax month.

In the case of class 2 contributions, the self employed person needs to register with a local DHSS office (on form CF11). His flat rate contributions can then be paid by purchasing contribution stamps to affix to a contribution card, or by direct debit through his bank account. It is important to note that if earnings are expected to be below the contribution threshold for class 2 contributions (£2,125 for 1987/88) the individual should apply for exemption since his liability to NIC continues unless he has a certificate of exemption.

Class 3 voluntary contributions may be paid in the same way as class 2 (i.e. by stamp or direct debit) or may be paid in a single sum at the end of the tax year.

Class 4 contributions are payable in the same way as income tax on the self-employed person's business profits. Normally, an income tax assessment is raised which includes a demand for class 4 NIC. Both the tax and the NIC will then usually be payable in two instalments – one half on 1 January in the relevant tax year and one half six months later. As this class of NIC is normally based on the same profits as are assessed to income tax, no separate records will be needed. There are, however, special rules where loss relief is claimed for income tax purposes.

What happens if an individual has more than one job?

A general principle is that an individual should not be liable to more than the maximum NIC payable if he were in a single class 1 employment. Thus an individual with two employments should pay no more than £1,407.15 for 1987/88.

An individual who is self-employed but also has part-time employment may qualify for a refund of, or, if he applies in advance, deferment of, all or part of class 2 and/or, class 4 contributions, under a formula which takes into account his total classes 1, 2 and 4 contributions paid or payable.

Where an individual has more than one job and expects to exceed his maximum contribution limit, he can apply in advance for 'deferment' of contributions. The DHSS may then confirm that no contributions need be deducted in one (or more) of the jobs.

There are no such limits on employers' (secondary) class 1 contributions. Thus each employer of an individual with more than one employment will continue to pay NIC as if it were the only employer.

Are contributions tax deductible?

An employer can deduct all his (secondary) class 1 contributions in computing taxable profits for income or corporation tax purposes. A self-employed person can deduct half of his class 4 contributions in arriving at his taxable income. However, an individual can obtain no tax relief for class 1, class 2 or class 3 contributions.

What do you receive for your contributions?

Entitlement to various forms of social security benefit is linked to the individual's record of contributions and for this purpose his class 1, 2 and 3 contributions may count. Class 4 contributions and the employer's class 1 contributions will not earn any form of benefit. (Reduced rate class 1 contributions payable by certain women under a pre 7 April 1977 election also do not count.)

The main 'contributory benefits' are the state retirement pension (for which class 1, 2 and 3 contributions can be taken into account) and unemployment benefits (for which only class 1 contributions can be taken into account). This means that the self-employed individual who has been paying only class 2 and 4 contributions will not qualify for unemployment benefit.

What is the relevance of 'contracted-out' employment?

If an employer has elected to contract out of the state earnings-related retirement scheme (SERPS) both employer and employee will then be entitled to pay lower amounts of class 1 contributions. By contracting out, the employer undertakes in effect to finance part of the state pension, thus relieving the state of part of its obligations. (A basic state pension remains directly payable by the state). To reflect this, a rebate of class 1 contributions is given to employer and employee. The standard rates given in Table 6.1 are 'rebated' by 4.1% (employer) and 2.15% (employee) but only on earnings between the lower and upper earnings limits (i.e. between £39 and £295 weekly earnings or £2,028 and £15,340 annual earnings).

Are there any ways of saving NIC?

In planning to save NIC, the possible impact on entitlement to benefits should be borne in mind.

Various deductions which can be taken into account for income tax/PAYE purposes such as pension contributions and personal allowances are not deductible in calculating earnings to which NIC applies. Therefore, a combination of a reduced salary and a non-contributory pension scheme should attract lower NIC liability than a higher salary with a contributory scheme.

Owing to the system of thresholds of rates, a small amount of extra pay can be more than offset by increased NIC. For example, an employee earning just £99.00 per week would suffer an extra £2 of NIC if his pay rose by £1. Conversely, a person earning a basic salary of say £200 per week might pay less NIC if his commissions or overtime were paid say quarterly rather than weekly. In the week in which the extra money is paid the ceiling on employee NIC liability may be exceeded, so that much of the extra payment would not suffer employee contributions. (If the extra pay was paid weekly, it might all attract NIC.) It should be noted, however, that the scope for planning in this way is limited by regulations.

Whilst the timing of payments during the year may affect employees' NIC liability, company directors are treated differently. Their liability is calculated on the basis of an 'annual earnings period'. Thus even if paid weekly or monthly, the annual thresholds and limits must be used. Consequently, employee NIC is levied on the first £15,340 of earnings paid to a director in 1987/88, rather than spread evenly over the whole year.

As benefits in kind do not normally attract NIC, a saving may be achieved by providing such benefits to employees instead of increasing cash salaries.

Dividends paid to shareholders are not 'earnings' for NIC purposes. Thus payment of dividends to employee shareholders, instead of salary, may save NIC.

There are complex rules in the legislation which are likely to affect many forms of NIC planning. For example, there are provisions to aggregate earnings from several related employments (to counter the possibility of splitting one job into several jobs, each of which is below the NIC threshold). There are also provisions to counteract avoidance by means of 'irregular' payment of earnings or 'abnormal' pay practices. The provision of benefits in place of salary and the strategy with regard to dividends and remuneration also require care.

7

Understanding Value Added Tax

What is VAT?

Value Added Tax is a tax which is levied by all European Community states, although rates in each country differ. VAT was first levied in the UK with effect from 1 April 1973 as one condition of our process of entry into the Common Market. Subsequent UK legislation has sought to reflect the planned harmonisation of Common Market VAT contained in various EEC directives. Further guidance is obtained from judgements of the European Court, as well as UK statutes, case law and VAT tribunal judgements.

VAT is a tax on the supply of goods and services made by a business in the UK; it is not a tax on income or profits. VAT is also payable on the importation of most goods and certain services into the UK. It is collected by businesses at all stages in the production and distribution chain and is ultimately borne by the final consumer. It is, therefore, a transaction tax. There are presently two rates of VAT, the standard rate of 15% and the zero-rate of 0%; supplies falling within these categories are known as 'taxable supplies'. Certain other supplies may be classified as exempt and are not liable to VAT. This distinction between zero-rated and exempt supplies may seem unnecessary since the VAT charged on both is nil, but it can be of crucial importance to 'partly exempt' businesses (see page 65).

VAT is levied according to the place of supply, rather than the residence of the person making the supply ('the taxpayer'). For example, if a UK trader has stock in both France and UK, the sale of goods in France will be subject to French TVA rather than UK VAT. There are rules for deciding the place where a supply takes place as well as rules for determining the time of that supply, which is also important.

Administration of VAT is the responsibility of the Commissioners of H M Customs & Excise, whose powers are wide-ranging. They may disclose information to other Government bodies, recover VAT through the courts and impose on businesses conditions, directions and requirements for records. An officer may enter and inspect your premises at a reasonable time, examine or remove your records and may obtain information from third parties, such as suppliers, customers or accountants.

In practice, officers of Customs & Excise exercise the majority of the Commissioners' powers. VAT policy matters are determined by headquarters offices and day to day local management is carried out by local VAT offices.

Must I register for VAT?

Registration for VAT is compulsory for individuals, partnerships and companies where business turnover of taxable supplies including VAT is expected to exceed £21,300 in the coming year or where it has exceeded £7,250 in the previous calendar quarter. 'Business' includes not only trades, professions or vocations but also clubs, societies and charities. You must notify a liability to register for VAT within 30 days, as failure to do so may render you liable to a penalty of 30% of the tax payable between the time you should have notified and the date that you did notify.

Where a business does not exceed the registration limit, it is possible to register voluntarily. A voluntary registration is permitted if only certain criteria are met and will be advantageous if sales are mainly to other VAT registered businesses. This is because you can recover VAT on purchases and your customers will usually be able to recover the VAT which you charge.

Since VAT is borne by the consumer who cannot reclaim VAT, small traders selling to the general public will usually benefit if they do not have to register and charge VAT. They will be unable to reclaim the VAT suffered on their purchases, but this cost can be passed on to the consumer, and VAT will not have to be charged on the mark-up or profit margin, thus enabling the small trader to charge a lower price to his customers.

Registration is made to your local VAT office using form VAT 1, which can be obtained from that office. You can have only one VAT registration for each legal entity, even if you carry on several different businesses. A VAT registration is allocated to a 'person' and, therefore, if separate registrations are required, separate legal entities must exist. Also, you cannot artificially divide your business into several component parts in order to stay below the VAT registration limits.

Since 1 April 1987, business receiving certain services from overseas have to take the value of those services into account when considering registration. If the value of these services exceeds the registration limit then Customs & Excise must be notified. The type of services involved include professional, advertising and financial services, but any business receiving international services should check whether the services received affect their VAT position.

I understand you can have just one VAT registration if you have several companies in your group. Is this likely to be of advantage to me?

If you have two or more companies under common control, you can elect to have a VAT group registration for all of the companies. As a result VAT is not due on any supplies between group companies contained in the registration. Care should be taken in selecting which companies should be included in the VAT group. The inclusion of a partially exempt or wholly exempt business will result in the group as a whole being considered partially exempt as all supplies made by a VAT group are deemed to be made through the representative member of the group, the company in whose name the group is registered for VAT.

The chief advantage arises from not charging VAT on intra-group supplies. This is particularly useful if one group company is unable to recover all its input tax. It also avoids the need to charge VAT on intra-group management charges and fees which would otherwise be taxable supplies. A VAT group has to submit only one VAT return for the group thereby minimising exposure to penalties from late payment of tax and submission of returns.

However, the collation of information from different sources may make timely returns difficult and adequate procedures should be set up in order to keep the advantage of submitting only one VAT return. Otherwise, exposure to penalties may be increased rather than diminished. You should also note that any VAT debt incurred by a company whilst it was a member of the VAT group may be recovered from other members even if the defaulting company has left the VAT group or been sold.

It is usually inappropriate to include a pension fund in a VAT group as Customs & Excise consider that all group members are jointly and severally liable. The risk to the fund's assets is potentially too great. Other companies that should not be grouped include any business that receives monthly repayments of VAT from Customs, for example an export company. The cashflow advantage would be lost if this type of business was included in a VAT group filing quarterly VAT returns.

In short, whether a VAT group will suit your particular business depends upon individual circumstances. However, you should consider this step as a means of saving tax if VAT on inter-company transactions is not fully recoverable by the recipient.

How do I pay VAT?

VAT is remitted to Customs on VAT returns, which are sent automatically to you from Customs VAT Central Unit at Southend just before your VAT period ends. A VAT return is laid out to show the tax on 'outputs' and on 'inputs'. Outputs are the goods or services you supply and inputs are the goods and services you purchase. Usually, the tax on outputs exceeds that on inputs and the excess is payable to Customs. However, in certain businesses such as exporters or retailers of zero-rated goods, input tax will exceed output tax, in which case Customs will repay the excess.

VAT periods are usually three months in length, although where regular VAT repayments are received, it is advantageous to make monthly returns. Returns must be submitted within 30 days of the end of your VAT period. Failure to do so may result in penalties ranging between 5% and 30% of the tax payable, depending upon the frequency of your default. Customs will allow a business to pay its VAT liability through the National Giro system, which effectively extends the payment date by seven extra days. Customs & Excise will need to authorise this method.

It is proposed from 1 October 1987, that businesses with an annual turnover including VAT of not more than £250,000 will be able to account for VAT on the basis of payments received and made, rather than on tax invoices received and issued. From mid 1988 smaller businesses will also be able to submit one annual return, which is preceded by nine equal instalments and accompanied by a 10th, balancing, payment. Also, you can have VAT returns which align with your financial year or internal accounting periods or both, if you wish.

What is a tax invoice and why is it important?

A tax invoice indicates the amount of VAT which you have been charged by your suppliers or establishes the amount of output tax which you charge to your customers. Except for retailers, you are required to issue a tax invoice to your customers and you must keep a duplicate.

There are rules governing the timing of the issue of a tax invoice, because it may establish a tax point. A tax point is the time at which output tax falls due to Customs. This is particularly important where a change in the rate of VAT is involved and in terms of cashflow because, in some circumstances, you may be able legitimately to delay the time at which you account for your output VAT. For example, your normal invoicing date may fall shortly before the end of your VAT period in which case you will effectively pay output tax to Customs within 30 days and probably before you receive payment. In some circumstances, it may be possible to delay invoicing until the beginning of your next VAT period, allowing you an extra three months to pay during which time you should have collected the output tax from your customers.

There are also certain minimum details which must be on the tax invoice, such as your VAT registration number, the rate of VAT and the type of goods or services supplied.

What records must I keep and for how long?

You must be able to demonstrate how you arrived at your output tax and input tax. You must keep your records for six years although Customs may, in certain circumstances, allow you to dispose of them before then, provided you obtain their prior approval. As a minimum, you must keep up to date records which show the amount of VAT which you have charged or for which you are liable, and records of the amount of VAT which you have paid. If you issue sales invoices you must keep copies. You must also retain original purchase invoices in order to substantiate your claims to input tax. In addition, you must keep a VAT account, which is a record of the VAT returns which you have submitted to Customs. The records do not have to be kept in a set way but must be in a form which will enable Customs officers to check the figures on your VAT return. Customs have the power to specify the records which must be kept if you fail to maintain proper standards.

When will Customs & Excise visit me?

Customs make periodic visits to check the accuracy of the VAT returns which you have submitted. The frequency is determined by Customs and may be as often as twice annually or as infrequent as once every five years or more and depends upon the type and size of business. The length of the visit will vary from half a day up to several weeks and again depends upon the complexity of your business.

There may be further visits which can be made for any reason. Customs will usually make their visits by pre-arranged appointment, except to resolve minor queries.

Customs will expect to see the owner, partner or director and the person responsible for completing the VAT returns and will expect to have all relevant documentation made available. They will check your records and will ask detailed questions on how you operate your business.

Can I appeal against a decision by Customs?

An appeal against a decision of Customs on certain matters may be made to a VAT tribunal. The appeal may proceed on a point of law to the High Court and continue up to the House of Lords. Matters on which an appeal to a VAT tribunal may be made are restricted and you must comply with certain conditions.

The first step is to ask your local VAT office to reconsider their decision. You may wish to provide further information or ask Customs to take into account the facts which may not have been fully considered. This does not affect your right of appeal to a VAT tribunal but it is not necessary to appeal to a VAT tribunal whilst this procedure is underway. Customs will normally discuss or review a case at any time, even though an appeal may already have been lodged with the VAT tribunal.

Is VAT payable on all transactions?

No. Firstly, the supply must be made by a person registered for VAT and it must be a standard-rated supply. A supply does not have to be made to a third party to attract VAT. For example, appropriation of goods for private use counts as a supply for VAT purposes and output tax must be accounted for at cost price although input tax may be reclaimed, subject to the normal rules.

Unless a supply is specifically zero-rated or exempt it is normally standard-rated. Certain income does not fall under any of those categories; for example, donations, which are outside the scope of VAT.

Those goods and services which are zero-rated or exempt are specified in VAT legislation. Examples of zero-rated supplies include food, export of goods, fuel and power and construction of new buildings. Exempt supplies include most other transactions and property, finance, insurance and health.

How do I calculate the VAT I must pay if I retail both standard-rated and zero-rated goods?

You can use any one of Retailers Schemes A to J or you can agree (in advance) any scheme which produces a reasonable reflection of the correct amount of tax due. The detail of each of the standard schemes varies and depends upon the size and nature of your business. For example, retail schemes H and J demand detailed accounting systems and are most often used by large retailers and schemes C, D and G have strict turnover limits.

You may only use a retail scheme if the nature of your business does not allow you to issue tax invoices for each sale. If only part of your business is retail you can use the retailer's scheme for that part and calculate tax due in the normal way for the rest of your supplies.

It is important to choose the correct scheme and to monitor turnover because failure to do so may mean you pay too much tax; for example, if you exceed the £200,000 turnover limit for scheme D (£500,000 from 1 October 1987), Customs may seek to impose scheme G which will mean you must add 12½% to the amount of tax you calculate as due under the scheme.

Can I claim back all the VAT I pay out?

Usually, provided it relates to your taxable supplies and has not been incurred for private purposes. If a registered person's supplies are not wholly taxable he may not be able to reclaim all of the input VAT which he pays out. There are also certain items of expenditure on which input VAT cannot be reclaimed, regardless of whether you make exempt supplies or whether they are for the purpose of the business. These include the purchase of a car and business entertainment.

Why is the distinction between zero-rated and exempt supplies relevant if no VAT is charged anyway?

If you make only zero-rated or standard-rated ('taxable') supplies, you can reclaim all of the input tax you have suffered. This is because the zero-rate is considered to be a rate of tax. Thus, the retailer of, for example, children's clothes can reclaim input VAT on his overheads even through VAT is not chargeable on his zero-rated supplies.

However, if all your supplies are exempt, you cannot register for VAT and, therefore, cannot reclaim any input tax.

What if I make both taxable and exempt supplies?

Many businesses will be in this position, in which case they are 'partly exempt'. The effect of making both taxable and exempt supplies is that you are not able to reclaim all of your input VAT, unless that input VAT relates to your taxable supplies. Input VAT relating to exempt supplies cannot be claimed unless it is within certain monetary limits or unless the supplies are of a type which may be ignored.

In this situation, it is necessary to adapt your accounting

system to identify input tax which relates directly to both taxable and exempt supplies. If you cannot directly relate input tax to supplies, you must apportion the remaining tax in a fair manner which should be agreed in advance with Customs. This is known as the 'standard-method' or 'direct attribution method'.

If you find you cannot attribute any of your input VAT or if attribution is impracticable, you can ask Customs to approve a special method, which is any method other than the standard-method which produces a fair result.

Partial exemption probably creates more problems in VAT than any other subject. Careful planning is necessary. Significant savings can be obtained as a result of judicious planning.

Example:

A partly exempt company wishes to build new premises. Although the construction of a new building is zero-rated, the company will not be able to recover input VAT incurred on legal and professional fees, architect's surveyor's or project management fees. However, if a subsidiary acquires the land, constructs the new building and grants a major interest (a lease in excess of 21 years or the freehold) to the parent it will create a zero-rated supply which should allow the subsidiary to register for VAT. As the subsidiary company will generate only taxable supplies, it will be able to reclaim input tax which the parent company would otherwise lose.

Do I charge VAT to overseas customers?

VAT is not chargeable on goods which you export from the UK. You must satisfy Customs that the goods have left the UK and you must keep supporting documentation such as certificates of shipment, insurance documents and correspondence. The provision of services to overseas customers may only be zero-rated in certain circumstances, such as services relating to land situated outside the UK or services connected with the export of goods.

Do I pay VAT on my imports?

VAT is payable on all goods which are imported into the UK, unless they are of a type which are zero-rated when supplied in the UK; for example, food. VAT is payable to Customs immediately, but there is a facility for VAT to be deferred by up to 30 days by arranging a bank guarantee. The import VAT is debited to your bank account on the 15th day of the succeeding month and may be reclaimed on the next VAT return which falls due.

Do I pay VAT on services supplied from overseas and how do I treat such services?

VAT is chargeable on some services supplied from abroad. Where such services are supplied by a person, who belongs in a country other than the UK, and are received by a taxable person who belongs in the UK for the purposes of any business carried on by him, the same consequences apply as if the taxable person had himself supplied the service in the UK, and that supply were a taxable supply. The relevant services include professional, advisory and advertising services and the secondment of staff. The payments to the overseas supplier for such services have to be converted into sterling and output VAT charged on the converted value. The net value of this supply is also to be included in the value of outputs on the VAT return. Of course the output VAT chargeable can also be treated as input tax and recovered in the normal way. This is called the 'reverse charge procedure'. It is designed to prevent unfair competition between an overseas supplier and one who belongs in the UK. For a fully taxable business i.e. one able to recover in full the VAT charged, the net effect of the reverse charge mechanism is nil (but the calculation must still be made). However it may create a tax cost where you make exempt as well as taxable supplies, due to the possible restriction in the recovery of input tax.

You say I must submit VAT returns within 30 days of the end of my VAT period – does this mean I have to pay VAT I charge to my customers before I receive it?

Yes, although you can reclaim input tax before you have paid it, provided you hold a tax invoice.

As already mentioned, from 1 October 1987, all businesses with a turnover of not more than £250,000 will be able to pay VAT they charge only when they receive it, provided they elect with Customs to do so. This also means you cannot reclaim input tax until you pay your suppliers.

Thus, businesses which pay suppliers some time before they receive payment from customers or businesses with a long sales credit period will benefit from cash accounting. Cash accounting also is guaranteed protection against having to pay VAT on bad debts, which under the present system may only be recovered if your customer becomes insolvent or bankrupt.

If you receive regular VAT repayments, for example because all of your supplies are zero-rated, you should not elect to use cash accounting as this will delay your recovery of input VAT.

What happens if I underpay VAT?

Until now, most errors involving underpaid tax have been adjusted with the issue of a VAT assessment by Customs. However, from 1989 all underpayments which can be assessed by Customs will be subject to interest, which is not deductible for corporation tax or income tax. There is already a default surcharge system for the late submission and payment of VAT returns as well as severe penalties for deliberate underpayments or overclaims of VAT. Penalties will also be imposed if your errors exceed certain prescribed limits, whether they are innocent errors or not. This underlines the need to ensure your procedures for submitting accurate and timely VAT returns are satisfactory.

Penalties currently in force are:

- failure to register on time – up to 30% of tax arrears;
- failure to retain records for 6 years – £500;
- unauthorised issue of tax invoices – up to 30% of tax charged;
- breaches of regulations – daily penalty, either £10, £20 or £30 depending on frequency of default;
- automatic civil penalty for 'dishonesty' – up to 100% of VAT evaded;
- default surcharge for late payment or late submission of VAT returns – from 5% to 30% of late tax, depending on frequency of default.

Penalties proposed for introduction in 1989:

- serious misdeclaration or neglect for significant underdeclarations – 30% of tax understated;
- interest on overdue tax.

- interest on overdue tax.

Can I claim back VAT I paid before I started trading or registered?

Yes, although there are time limits and certain conditions. Input VAT on goods may be reclaimed only if those goods are on hand at the time of registration. You will have to prove this to Customs by compiling a stock account. However, services which have been purchased up to six months before you started trading or registered for VAT may be reclaimed provided you hold the proper documentation. Certain other conditions are imposed where the expenditure has been incurred on behalf of companies prior to their incorporation.

What if I pay VAT in other countries?

If you pay VAT in other member states of the European Community you may be able to recover it from the country concerned provided you do not have a business establishment or make VAT supplies in that country. You must abide by the rules laid down by that country and there are strict time limits for submitting a claim. Not all VAT incurred may be reclaimable, as you will be subject to the rules in force for VAT registered traders in that member state.

What happens if I cease to trade?

If your cessation is temporary, your VAT registration can continue until you recommence your business. If, however, your cessation is permanent you must notify Customs and deregister from VAT. You have 30 days to notify Customs and there are daily penalties, ranging from £10 to £30, for failing to do so.

If there are stocks and other business assets on hand at the time of your deregistration you are liable to pay Customs output tax on the value of those items on hand unless the tax amounts to less than £250. If, however, you transfer your business to a going concern, to a person who is already registered or becomes liable to be registered as a result of the transfer you can not charge VAT as the transfer is regarded as outside the scope of VAT.

Why must I not charge VAT if I transfer my business as a going concern?

Because no supply takes place, it is in the interests of both vendor and purchasers to establish whether a transfer of a going concern takes place.

If you are a vendor and do not charge VAT and if the sale *is not* a transfer you will have to pay VAT to Customs that you may not be able to recover from the purchaser. If you are a purchaser and have paid VAT and if the sale *is* a transfer you cannot recover the VAT from Customs as input tax. Thus, if you are a vendor you may receive less than the value of your business. If you are a purchaser you may pay more than you need.

What happens if I change the organisation of my business?

You are required to notify changes of your business to Customs. Some changes will require a new VAT registration; for example, a change from a sole proprietorship to a company or partnership. Others, such as change of address or addition of a partner to an existing partnership, do not require a new registration but must be notified to Customs promptly. Again, there are penalties for failure to do so.

What about customs duties?

If you import goods from outside the UK for your business, you may well have to pay customs duty at import. This is yet another form of taxation, a tax on imports, and it should not be treated as an unavoidable or inevitable tax. There are a number of ways of reducing or even eliminating this tax, and where it must be paid, there are ways of delaying payment, or of easing the administrative burden of importing.

Before you import goods you should consider whether you can take advantage of any of the wide variety of duty reliefs available. There are reliefs for goods imported to be re-exported later, goods imported temporarily for use, for goods re-imported after being exported previously, and in many other circumstances. But remember, to claim the relief you must usually apply to Customs for an authorisation *in advance*.

You should also consider whether you might benefit from

some of the simplifications for imports, such as customs warehousing, free zones, or duty deferment. These can help to delay the duty and VAT due at the time of import. They can also make importing easier since you can control not only when you pay the duty and VAT, but also when you have your goods.

The secret of success in this complex area is to plan ahead, and to be aware of the opportunities available. It's all a matter of knowing which way to turn.

Some 'dos' and 'don'ts' in saving VAT

Do
- register on time;
- consider voluntary registration;
- consider a VAT group registration;
- submit your VAT returns on time;
- consider monthly VAT returns (repayment businesses only);
- consider annual VAT returns and/or cash accounting if your turnover is not more than £250,000 (from 1 October 1987);
- keep duplicate sales invoices; original purchase invoices;
- consider delaying issue of tax invoices, where the date falls around the end of your VAT period;
- maintain adequate VAT records and retain them for 6 years;
- establish the correct VAT liability of your supplies;
- choose the most appropriate retail scheme (retailers only);
- choose the most beneficial partial exemption method;
- retain evidence of exported goods and imported goods;
- consider VAT deferment for imported goods.
- *Remember penalties*!

Don't
- forget to ensure your VAT procedures are adequate;
- accept all Customs decisions – they can be wrong too!
- forget to claim input tax incurred prior to trading or registration;
- forget to recover VAT paid in other EEC states;
- charge VAT if you sell your business as a going concern;
- pay VAT if you acquire a business as a going concern;
- forget to inform Customs of changes to your business particulars;
- forget the fuel scale benefit for private fuel;
- *forget penalties*!

8

Tax Saving for Directors and Employees

What is my responsibility for tax on employee salaries?

All employees are subject to tax under Schedule E on their income from employment. The law imposes upon the employer responsibility under the Pay As You Earn (PAYE) system for deducting Schedule E income tax from all payments of wages, salaries or other remuneration, and paying the tax over to the Inland Revenue. Payment of National Insurance contributions (NIC) as part of the PAYE system is compulsory under the Social Security Acts (see chapter 6). The PAYE branch of the Inland Revenue and the DHSS issue full instructions to employers for calculating PAYE and NIC deductions whenever remuneration is paid and for reporting expenses and benefits paid to employees (see page 83). These are the Employer's Guide to PAYE and the Employer's Guide to NIC (NP15) which are essential reading for an employer.

PAYE applies not only to regular wages and salaries but also to:

- directors' fees and cash drawings, including amounts credited to accounts which directors have with the company;
- wages and salaries etc of directors' or sole traders' spouses;
- most payments to casual or temporary labour;
- benefits paid in cash, for example the cost of travel from home to work;
- expenses allowances and other payments if they are not covered in full by deductible business expenses.

The Inland Revenue are nowadays devoting more resources to enforcing the PAYE rules.

Rules for deducting tax similar to PAYE may apply to payments to contractors and sub-contractors in the building industry.

You have said that I should operate PAYE and NIC on payments to my employees but there are some people who provide services to my company who have said that they are self-employed – should I deduct PAYE and NIC from payments made to them?

The distinction between an employee working under a contract of service and a self employed person providing services to the company can often be a fine one. Moreover, the authorities do not always agree on a worker's status so that, for example, registration for value added tax is not conclusive that PAYE and NIC are not applicable. Before payments to any individual are excluded from your payroll you should be absolutely sure that the recipient could not be considered to be an employee. If you have any doubts on the matter you should seek professional advice and/or contact your own Inspector of Taxes before making payments without deductions of PAYE and NIC. This is important as if it subsequently transpires that payments made free of deductions should have been included in your payroll, the authorities will normally seek to recover the deduction which should have been made from the employer and not from the recipient and the employer's ability to recover anything from the recipient will be severely limited in many cases.

Some people who work for you might be paid by someone else, for example, people who are paid by an agency, where you pay fees to the agency. Whenever this happens, you should ask the person who pays the worker to confirm in writing that he is operating PAYE, whether or not the worker says he is self-employed. If he is not, you might be liable even though you are not paying the worker. If the person paying the worker is outside the UK, you should always obtain professional advice. You should operate PAYE on any payments which you make.

Payments to casual or temporary workers are commonly a source of error. The Employer's Guide to PAYE has very detailed rules to be applied where you pay somebody for the first time, and you should always follow these rigidly.

When do I have to pay over the PAYE to the Collector of Taxes?

Amounts of PAYE and NIC due have to be paid to the Collector of Taxes within 14 days of the end of an income tax month. Income tax months end on the fifth day of a calendar month. The amounts due are the amounts of income tax and primary NIC which should have been deducted from emoluments paid in the month (if the regulations were properly applied) and secondary NIC on those emoluments. (See chapter 6 on computing NIC)

Sometimes it is not certain when emoluments are paid, and the Employer's Guide gives advice on various items, for example, advances and holiday pay. Payment might effectively be made in some cases before a director or employee receives cash. For example, a sum credited to a director's account with his company would be paid if he can draw on the account at will, or if an amount is set off against money he owes to the company.

What are statutory sick pay and statutory maternity pay and must I operate them?

Statutory sick pay (SSP) is paid by the employer in respect of most employees where average earnings equal or exceed the lower weekly earnings limit for NIC liability. It is paid for the first twenty-eight weeks of an employee's sick pay entitlement in a tax year, after which the employee can claim State Sickness Benefit. The employer may deduct payments of SSP from his liability to account for NIC and PAYE deductions. In addition, an employer who has paid SSP may obtain a further rebate from NIC. SSP is itself subject to PAYE and NIC.

Statutory maternity pay (SMP) was introduced on 6 April 1987. It applies where the baby was expected to be born on or after 26 June 1987. As for SSP, payments are made by the employer but he can recover them by setting them off against liability to account for PAYE and NIC deductions. However, the qualifying conditions for SMP and the period for which it is payable vary considerably from those for SSP. Broadly, SMP is only payable to women who have two years service and whose pay during a six month period equalled or exceeded the lower earnings limit for NIC purposes. It is payable for a minimum of 18 weeks and it is liable both to income tax and NIC (under the PAYE system).

Operating the SSP and SMP system gives the employer an additional administrative burden in keeping records of employee sickness, maternity and their entitlements to the payments. Full details of the systems are provided to employers by the Department of Health and Social Security (DHSS).

Are emoluments taxed in the year in which they are paid?

The income tax deducted by an employer under PAYE is calculated on payments and the deduction is made when the emoluments are paid. However, PAYE is only a means of collection. Although there are exceptions, the income tax charged on a director or employee on his emoluments is assessed for the income tax year in which he does the work for which he earns the emoluments. In most cases, this will be the same as the year of payment, but differences arise, for example, with bonuses and commission.

For example, if a bonus is paid in March 1988 for the calendar year 1987, in the sum of £16,000, PAYE will be deducted in the year 1987/88 using the PAYE code, tax table and other emoluments for the year 1987/88. However, the bonus will be assessable as to one quarter (January to March 1987) for the year 1986/87 (£4,000) and three quarters (April to December 1987) for the year 1987/88 (£12,000). Depending on the amounts and incidence of bonuses for other periods, the result may be that the assessments on the employee for the year 1986/87 may show underpayments and the assessments for the year 1986/87 could not be finalised until May 1988.

In circumstances such as these, the employee or the Inland Revenue may request a non-statutory 'accounts basis' for assessment purposes. PAYE is unaffected. On the accounts basis, the earnings for an income tax year are taken to be those shown in the accounts ending in the year. In the example above, if the employer's accounting period was a calendar year, the bonus (and all other emoluments shown in the accounts) would be assessed for the year 1987/88, and the timing differences eliminated.

Special adjustments are required when the accounts basis is first adopted and when the employment or directorship ceases and if there are changes in the employer's accounting date. Since these have the effect of taxing some emoluments more than once and others not at all, the decision whether to request or accept an accounts basis requires careful consideration. In practice, there are variations in the kind of accounts basis used.

NIC is always computed on amounts paid and the use of an accounts basis for income tax will not affect the amounts due.

Are there still tax advantages in giving employees benefits rather than extra salary?

Employees usually prefer to receive cash which they are free to spend rather than a benefit which may have less value to them than its real cost. Employers can, however, often obtain advantageous group discount terms for their employees, and certain benefits can be provided to employees on advantageous tax terms, including:

- canteen meals;
- use of cars and car fuel;
- use of other assets, such as clothing or furniture;
- removal expenses, where a move is required for the employment;
- medical insurance for lower-paid employees who are not directors;
- shares under approved option or profit sharing schemes (see chapter 9);
- pensions (see chapters 10 and 11);
- payments on termination of employment;
- small loans;
- living accommodation.

In addition NIC would not be payable on some of these benefits. NIC considerations on payments and benefits generally are dealt with on page 83.

What are the rules for taxing benefits?

Benefits are normally taxable as part of the earnings from an employment under Schedule E. The general rule is that the benefit taxable upon an employee is the 'money's worth' of the benefit in his or her hands. If, for example, a company settles an employee's private expenses of £100, he is treated as receiving £100 income. If it gives him a television set, he is taxed on what he could resell the television for. If the company allows him to use the television but continues to own it and assuming that the employee cannot hire it to someone else or exchange it for more salary, he will have no taxable benefit.

For higher-paid employees (those with earnings plus benefits and reimbursed expenses at an annual rate of £8,500 or more) and directors, there is a more stringent rule for calculating taxable benefits. This rule is that benefits provided to them or their families by virtue of their employment are taxable on the basis of either the cost to the company or money's worth to the employee, whichever is the greater, or where the benefit is the use of an asset on the basis of an annual value. The main exceptions to this rule are for dining facilities provided for staff generally, which are tax-free, and company cars which are taxed at statutory rates below the normal cost of owning and running the car.

Certain benefits are taxable on all employees under standard rules whether or not they are directors or in the higher-paid category. These include vouchers exchangeable for goods and services, purchases by an employer's credit card, travel tickets, living accommodation, and payments on the termination of employment.

The normal basis of charge for the more common employee benefits is summarised in Table 8.1, showing separately the charge upon higher-paid employees and directors and upon other employees.

Table 8.1 *Tax charge on common employee benefits*

Benefit	Tax charge for directors and higher paid employees	Tax charge for other employees
Meals provided directly for all employees by employer on own premises	Tax free	Tax free
Cars owned or leased by employer and made available to employees or members of their families for private use	Scale benefit (a)	Tax free (g)

Table 8.1 *continued*

Petrol (or diesel) made available by employer	Scale benefit (a)	Special rules (a)
Other assets made available for use of employees or members of their families	20% of market value plus expenses	Tax free (g)
Reasonable removal expenses caused by employment	Tax free	Tax free
Loans at favourable interest rates	Notional interest (b)	Tax free (g)
Vouchers for cash, goods or services	Cost	Cost
Purchases by company credit cards	Cost of purchases	Cost of purchases
Travel tickets (non-business)	Cost	Cost
Medical insurance	Cost	Tax free
Living accommodation	Annual value (or rent paid by employer if higher) plus private expenses, if any (c)	Annual value (or rent paid by employer if higher) plus private expenses, if any (c)
Pensions	Tax free (d)	Tax free (d)
Life assurance	Tax free (d)	Tax free (d)
Shares under approved schemes	Special rules (e)	Special rules (e)
Payments on termination of employment	Low tax (f)	Low tax (f)

Notes

(a) The following section deals with taxation of company cars.
(b) There is a minimum amount of £200 up to which notional interest is not assessed, and interest on which the employee could claim tax relief is not assessed.
(c) Where the cost of the property (or in some cases its value) exceeds £75,000 the taxable benefit is further increased.
(d) Scheme must be approved by Inland Revenue (see page 105).
(e) See chapter 9.
(f) See page 81.
(g) If the employee can make money from the asset or there is a quid pro quo in terms of salary, bonuses etc., the benefit may be taxable.

What are the main rules for taxing company cars?

The main rules for calculating the benefit for the year to 5 April 1988 are as follows.

- Higher paid employees and directors are assessed according to a table of charges (see Table 8.2), the benefit varying according to age, cost and engine size of car.

- Employees who are neither directors nor higher-paid are not assessed to the scale charge. They will however be assessed if their private expenses are met by the employer, or they use company credit cards, or vouchers, or can turn the benefit into money in some way, for example, extra salary for giving up the car.

- There is no assessment upon the use of 'pooled cars' but the qualifying rules are narrowly drawn.

- The car benefit is reduced by any amount an employee is required to pay as a condition of the car being available for his private use.

- An additional scale charge is made in respect of private fuel provided for higher-paid employees and directors with company cars. Other employees will be assessed on any expenditure on car fuel used for private mileage which is met by reimbursement, the settlement of the employee's own liability, by the issue of vouchers or by a company credit card.

- Reimbursement of the cost of fuel for private mileage for all employees is liable to NIC.

Table 8.2 *Directors and higher-paid employees: scale charges for company cars – year to 5 April 1988.*

	Age of car at end of tax year	
	Under 4 years	4 years or more
(A) Original market value up to £19,250 cylinder capacity:		
– 1400cc or less	£525	£350
–1400 – 2000cc	£700	£470
– more than 2000cc	£1,100	£725
(B) Original market value over £19,250		
–£19,251 – £29,000	£1,450	£970
–more than £29,000	£2,300	£1,530

Notes

The scale benefits from Table 8.2 are charged at three levels according to the business mileage of the employee during the year:

- at least 18,000 business miles – half scale charge;
- 2,501 – 17,999 business miles – scale charge;
- 2,500 or fewer miles – scale charge plus half;
- 'second' cars are assessed at scale charge plus half whether or not business mileage is more than 2,500 miles.

Table 8.3 *Directors and higher-paid employees: scale charges for car fuel – year to 5 April 1988*

Cylinder capacity:	
1400cc or less	£480
1401 – 2000cc	£600
more than 2000cc	£900

Notes
- The fuel charge applies for each car provided. It applies in full unless the employee either pays for all private fuel or receives fuel for only business mileage.
- Where the employee travels at least 18,000 business miles, so that the car benefit is half the scale charge, the fuel scale charge is also reduced to half.

Reductions in the car scale and fuel scale charges are also made when a car is unavailable for certain periods.

Where petrol is provided for employees' private mileage in a VAT return period, the employer must account for VAT on an appropriate proportion of the fuel scale charges used for income tax for each car.

A 'Company car tax guide' written by Coopers & Lybrand is available from Tolleys (price £4.25).

My company pays a mileage allowance to employees who use their own cars on business – do we have to report this to the Inland Revenue?

Yes. It is essential to agree with the Inland Revenue that the allowance does no more than cover reasonable business expenses. Otherwise, such payments may be earnings for which the company would have to account for PAYE and NIC.

Can the company provide loans to employees?

There are restrictions which, for two categories of individuals, will either prohibit the making of loans or result in tax penalties.

- Company directors – it is illegal in most circumstances for a company to make loans to its directors.
- Company shareholders – a close company must in nearly all cases pay to the Inland Revenue an amount equal to advance corporation tax (27/73) on making a loan to a shareholder or to one of his or her 'associates', a term which includes most members of the shareholder's family.

For higher-paid employees, and directors, the benefit of a loan at a low or nil rate of interest is calculated as the interest on the loan at the 'official rate' less interest if any paid. The official rate varies from time to time. The benefit is not taxed if it (or the aggregate benefit if there is more than one loan) does not exceed £200 or if the loan is used for a qualifying purpose (for example the purchase of a main residence). For other employees, the benefit of a loan at a low rate or nil rate of interest is not taxed. For any employee, however, the waiver or release of a loan, irrespective of the rate of interest, may be taxable as employment income.

What are the current rules for taxing payments on termination of employment?

All payments made to employees on the termination of the holding of an office or employment, or any change in its functions, are charged to Schedule E tax, but a favourable basis might apply. The favourable basis described below only applies to payments not otherwise charged to income tax in full. For instance, if the payment is a reward or bonus for past services or if the individual has some entitlement to it from his or her contract of service, it will be fully chargeable to tax as Schedule E income. A payment made to compensate the holder of a service contract on terminating his employment will normally rank for the favourable treatment. Payments to shareholders may be taxable as dividends, and advice should be taken in such cases.

Arrangements set up in advance to make lump sum payments on termination of an employment are best avoided, but the Inland Revenue has stated that in normal cases of redundancy it will accept a bona fide termination payment as such, and it invites employers to seek advance clearance in cases of doubt.

Where the favourable basis for taxing termination payments applies the income tax chargeable is as follows.

Slice of termination payment	Income tax chargeable
(£)	(£)
0 – 25,000	exempt
25,001 – 50,000	tax less 50%
50,001 – 75,000	tax less 25%
75,001 and above	taxable in full

Special rules apply where there is more than one payment or more than one termination etc. More favourable rules can apply in special cases, for example where the payment is made following death or injury or in respect of foreign service.

The employer is responsible for deducting tax on a termination payment under the PAYE system. Where the favourable basis applies, the £25,000 exemption can be taken into account if it is due, but the employer can only have regard to the other reliefs if the Inland Revenue agrees. The employer will normally obtain tax relief for the gross payment as an expense of the trade unless it was not paid for the purposes of the trade, for example, in connection with a takeover or for family reasons.

Do the same rules for taxing benefits apply both to employees of a company and to employees of an individual or partnership?

Yes. The same rules apply in taxing employee benefits and in relation to employee pension schemes. Employee share schemes necessarily require that the employer is a company. Remember that the partners in a partnership are not employees. The benefits and expenses of sole traders and partners are covered on pages 11–13.

What are the general rules for deducting business expenses?

The rules are notoriously rigid and narrow, and it is fair comment that the deductibility of many expenses owes much to the flexibility of the Inland Revenue which, however, is becoming less apparent in many cases.

All expenses must be necessary. This means that doing the job requires the expense to be incurred. In this respect, you have to distinguish the employer's requirements from those of the job. For example, requiring an employee to join a Club, or to live in a particular place will not guarantee a deduction if doing the work does not require it.

Expenses must also be incurred in the performance of the duties of the job. This rule precludes home to office travel and causes difficulties for employees who are based, for example, on a customer's premises for periods of time.

In addition, expenses other than travel must be wholly and exclusively incurred for business purposes. If there is a dual purpose, the expense cannot be deducted. For this reason, telephone rentals and personal clothing are likely to be precluded, and other expenses, such as visits to Wimbledon, the theatre and football matches may be uncertain (for guests also).

The Inland Revenue look closely at expenses. In particular, the expenses of spouses accompanying their husbands or wives on business journeys and on other occasions will often fail to satisfy the tests and can colour the husband's or wife's expense. The Inland Revenue give some guidance in their booklet 480 but professional advice is desirable in this area.

The annual return of expenses and benefits for directors and higher-paid employees on form P11D is a chore – can the work be reduced?

Yes. The Inland Revenue can give an employer dispensations from returning certain expense payments and benefits where the employer can show that there will be no charge to tax in respect of those payments. The most frequent case is the reimbursement of travel expenses, which will normally not give rise to a benefit.

A dispensation will save effort, but will only be given if the Inland Revenue is satisfied that the company's system of control is adequate to ensure that no tax liability arises. The Inland Revenue often ask searching questions about the company's procedures and benefit lists and may decide to carry out a review if a dispensation is requested. Where company credit cards and vouchers are used to meet expenses, separate dispensations are required.

Do the same rules apply for calculation of NIC?

Most non-cash benefits will not create any liability to NIC either for the employee or the employer. This is an important consideration to bear in mind. Given the current rates of employee and employer contributions (see page 53) significant savings of NIC can be made by providing benefits other than in cash.

However, it is equally important to understand that there are payments which can attract an NIC liability which would not attract a tax liability or would not immediately be subject to PAYE. For example, whilst PAYE is operated on net pay after deductions of contributions to an approved company pension scheme, NIC is calculated on the gross amount of earnings. The Employer's Guide to NIC (NP 15) sets out details of benefits and other payments which are outside the scope of NIC.

9

Share Schemes and Profit Sharing

What do these terms mean?

'Share schemes' refer to the various ways in which employees and directors may be given a stake in the company or group for which they work. This stake may be by way of direct share ownership or by having the right (option) to purchase shares. Share schemes for employees and directors tend to be treated harshly under UK tax rules, as if any gains were income from the employment. However, there are several kinds of employee share schemes which can be 'approved' by the Inland Revenue resulting in more favourable tax treatment, and these schemes are being introduced by many employers.

'Profit Related Pay' (PRP) in its widest sense encompasses not only the PRP provisions of Finance (No 2) Act 1987 (see below) but also cash bonus systems by means of which employees and directors may participate in the profitability of their employer. Such cash bonuses are treated, for tax purposes, as part of salary in the normal way and whilst they have a place in focusing the attention of employees and directors on the profitability of the business, there are no particular tax implications to be considered. In the remainder of this chapter the term PRP refers to an employees' scheme registered under the 1987 legislation by means of which a proportion of earnings can be received free of income tax.

What types of business entity can operate share schemes or PRP?

Clearly, Share Schemes can only be operated by companies with share capital. Share Schemes can be and are successfully run by private companies as well as by public companies which are quoted on a stock market. Private companies do however have the additional task of setting a value on their shares. PRP can be operated by any business whether company, sole trader or partnership. Sole traders and partnerships may be unwilling to disclose their profit figures, but PRP need not relate to the profit achieved by the whole business as its operation can be restricted to one or more employment units within the business, provided audited accounts can be produced.

Is it a good idea for a company to introduce a share scheme?

A share scheme is not a substitute for a properly structured remuneration policy but it can play a useful part. Ideally it should be introduced as part of a more comprehensive programme concerned with employee communication and involvement. Companies which have introduced share schemes list among their reasons for doing so:

- encouraging employees to have a common interest with the shareholders;
- the tax efficient nature of an Inland Revenue approved share scheme;
- as regards senior employees, the fact that share options are expected by many ambitious employees to be part of their remuneration package; and
- particularly with senior employees, a sharing of the benefits of improved company performance which will encourage such employees to stay with a successful company.

In what ways are approved share schemes more tax efficient than unapproved share schemes?

Share schemes, both approved and unapproved, fall into two basic types. There are those schemes under which shares are provided to employees either free or for a price up to the market value price. Secondly there are a variety of option schemes under which the employees are granted a right (option) to purchase shares.

If a share scheme does not have Inland Revenue approval, a charge to income tax can arise in one or more of the following circumstances:

- at the date of grant of an option to purchase shares if the option is capable of exercise for 7 years or longer. In this case the income tax charge could be based on the difference between the market value of the shares at the date of grant and the price which the employee is obliged to pay for them;
- on the date of the exercise of the share option. In this case the income tax charge is based on the difference between the value of the shares at the date of exercise of the share option less the aggregate of the price paid for the shares, the option and any amount taxed on the grant;
- where shares are received by an employee at less than market value, then depending on the circumstances there will be an income tax charge on the discount which he has enjoyed, or the discount will be treated as a notional loan outstanding to him which will give rise to a tax charge based on the interest which would have been paid commercially on a loan of that size. In the event that the employee sells the shares, this notional 'loan' is treated as income received; and
- unless the share ownership in the company satisfies certain complex conditions and the employee's shares are free from restrictions, there could be a charge to income tax on the growth in value of the shares over the period that the employee owns them.

By contrast, if shares are acquired under an approved share option scheme, the only tax charge on an employee will be a charge to capital gains tax when he finally sells the shares. Income tax can of course be charged up to the full marginal rate of 60% whereas capital gains tax is at 30% after deducting the annual exempt amount (£6,600 for 1987/88) and the indexation allowance to take into account inflation over the period that the shares are owned by the employee.

What types of approved share schemes are available?

There are three basic types:

- The Finance Act 1978 Approved Profit Sharing Scheme;
- The Finance Act 1980 Approved Option Linked Save-As-You-Earn (SAYE) or 'Share Save' Scheme; and
- The Finance Act 1984 Approved Share Option Scheme, often referred to as the Executive Share Option Scheme (although participation need not be limited to executives).

The profit sharing scheme and the SAYE Scheme are broad based schemes in that they must be open to substantially all full time employees, whereas participation in the executive share option scheme can be limited to employees selected by the directors.

A more detailed account of employee share schemes may be found in the book *Employee Share Schemes in Practice*, by Coopers & Lybrand and Monks Publications available from Monks Publications, Debden Green, Saffron Walden, Essex, CB11 3LX, price £40.

How does the profit sharing scheme work?

The scheme must be open to all full time employees with five years service, although part timers and other employees with less than five year's service may be included. Employees must participate on similar terms but the level of participation can vary by reference to such factors as pay, seniority and length of service.

The scheme provides for a trust to be set up to purchase and hold the shares for the benefit of employees. Each year the company will make a payment to the trustees, this payment being deductible for corporation tax purposes. The size of the payment is normally calculated by reference to a formula. The trustees will buy shares or subscribe for newly issued shares which are then allocated to each employee who participates. The shares must be held by the trustees for two years but will normally be held for five years if the full income tax advantages are to be enjoyed by the employee. The employee can ask for his shares to be transferred to him or he can sell his shares to the trustees at any time after the first two years, but if he does so before five years have elapsed he will suffer an income tax charge on either 100% or 75% of the value of the shares when they were allocated to him. If the shares have fallen below this value the income tax charge will be based on the lower value. After five years the employee can receive the shares completely free of income tax.

The maximum value of shares which may be allocated to an employee in any tax year is restricted to the greater of £1,250 or 10% of earnings (with an upper limit of £5,000).

A scheme may offer the employee the choice of shares or a cash bonus. Since a cash bonus would be subject to tax and national insurance contributions, whereas the shares would not be, there is a strong incentive for an employee to opt for shares rather than cash.

Another alternative is to provide an employee with one (or more) 'free' shares under an approved profit sharing scheme for each share purchased out of his own resources. Often the employee will purchase his shares from monthly deductions from his pay.

An example of how a typical approved profit sharing scheme might operate is set out below:

John Hacker has been employed by Complexsoft Limited for three years which is the qualifying period under the company's profit sharing scheme. He is invited to participate. It is a 'cash alternative' scheme which means that if he elects not to participate in the profit sharing scheme, he will be paid a cash bonus.

He chooses to participate. He signs the appropriate form and agrees to be bound by the terms of the scheme.

The board of Complexsoft Limited meet to determine the profit share allocation. Having reviewed the results for the year and the practice in the previous year, they decide to set aside £350,000 for the profit sharing scheme. This is about 4% of pre-tax profits.

The total sum set aside is divided by the total earnings bill for all eligible employees. As a result of this calculation, every participating employee is notionally allocated participation worth 5.25% of earnings.

John earned £15,000 last year. Out of the sum paid by the company to the scheme trustees, the trustees acquire £787.50 of new shares on John's behalf.

For the next two years the shares have to be held by the trustees, although John will receive dividends and will be asked to tell the trustees how his shares should be voted.

After two years John may obtain direct control of the shares and sell them. However, if he wants to avoid any income tax liability, he will have to leave the shares with the trustees for five years.

In conclusion, compared to the other approved schemes available, the profit sharing scheme is the only one which will immediately put employees into the same position as a shareholder. The employee will suffer the risks and enjoy the rewards of share ownership and will receive any dividends which are declared.

A profit sharing scheme with no cash alternative will result in virtually all eligible members of the work force becoming shareholders, compared to the likely take up rate of 15–20% of the SAYE scheme (see below).

Provided that an employee waits the full five years before owning the shares directly, the only tax charge which he will suffer as a result of participating in the scheme will be a capital gains tax charge when he sells the shares, based on the net sale proceeds less the market value of the shares at the time when they were first allocated to him by the trustees.

A profit sharing scheme can be useful for the shareholders of a private company who wish to realise some of their equity. Not only can the shareholders sell shares to the trustees, but the company gets a tax deduction for the funds given to the trustees for the purchases.

Disadvantages include the administration involved and the ongoing cost of running the trust.

Profit sharing schemes are the least popular of the approved schemes available, but they are successfully operated by quoted and private companies alike. Companies which have instituted profit sharing schemes and employees of such companies are often agreed that these schemes contribute to company success.

What are the key features of the Save-As-You-Earn linked share option scheme?

Like the approved profit sharing scheme, the scheme must be open to all full time employees with five years service, although individual part timers and other employees with less than five years service may participate at the company's discretion. As the name suggests, the scheme is a form of share option scheme. The company grants participants an option to purchase company shares usually at 90% of the current market value. Unless the company shares are quoted on a national stock exchange, the market value must be agreed with the Inland Revenue before options are granted.

The option is usually capable of exercise after five years but can be capable of exercise after seven years depending on the scheme rules. An employee wishing to participate must agree to enter a SAYE contract, typically operated by a building society but a National Savings contract is also possible. He must agree to save from his salary a regular monthly or weekly amount which can be up to a maximum of £100 per month. Once set the monthly or weekly amount cannot be varied but additional SAYE contracts can be taken out if offered by the company. Should the payments not be kept up then the contract is cancelled, the option lapses and the employee's savings are returned to him with any accrued interest.

Under the SAYE rules the amount which the employee saves qualifies for a tax free bonus after five years or after seven years and the savings plus the accrued bonus is calculated to be sufficient to pay for the number of shares over which options have been granted. At the relevant time the employee is given six months to decide whether to exercise his options or have his savings returned to him with the tax free bonus. Where the contract was originally for five years, at the five year point he could either exercise his options or allow his options to lapse and leave his savings with the building society to qualify for a higher tax free bonus after a further 2 years.

The company can choose whether to provide for exercise at the five year point or the seven year point or to give the employee the choice when he enters the contract. The company can also decide whether or not accrued bonuses will augment the sum available to exercise options.

Following the enactment of the Finance Act 1987, in the event of a takeover and providing that the acquiring company agrees, it is possible for an employee to substitute options over the new company's shares for the options over the old company's shares. Provided that the qualifying conditions are met, the new options will qualify for favourable tax treatment on exercise.

An example of how a typical scheme might operate is set out below:

Peter James, a laboratory technician with Hazard Chemicals Limited for five years, was sent details of his company's SAYE Share Option Scheme. After attending a meeting in the works canteen at which the scheme was explained, he decided to join the scheme.

Peter agreed to save £20 per month for five years. At the end of the five year period he will have saved £1,200. The building society with which he saves will give him a tax free bonus equal to 12 months contributions. This will make the total sum available to him at the end of five years £1,440.

At the same time Peter was granted an option over £1,584 worth of company shares. The shares were valued at 110p about ten days before Peter made his decision. The option price for the shares under Peter's option contract was 100p, about 90% of the market price.

A SAYE scheme is an economical way of allowing employees to share in their company's growth in value. The scheme is relatively simple to operate and the major building societies are all prepared to assist with the printing of literature and with employee communication by means of presentations and videos. It must be borne in mind however that the likely level of participation will often be relatively low, perhaps in the order of 15–20% and will tend to be confined to those with freely disposable income such as middle management or above and single people or dual income couples.

From the employee's point of view, if the share value fails to rise, he will not lose, but instead of exercising the option will receive a reasonable return on his savings. As with all approved schemes the employee, under normal circumstances, will suffer no charge to income tax as a result of participation. The only charge will be a capital gains tax charge on the sale of any shares which he decides to acquire by exercising his options. The charge is based on the difference between the sale proceeds and the price which he paid for the shares, less the annual exempt amount (£6,600 for 1987/88) and any indexation allowance to take account of inflation over the period he has owned the shares. Potentially the rewards can be significant should the shares perform well.

Directors often feel it to be appropriate to introduce a SAYE scheme simultaneously with the introduction of an approved executive share option scheme.

How does an approved executive share option scheme work?

An individual's participation in such a scheme is entirely at the discretion of the board of directors. Although often termed the executive share option scheme, participation need not be so limited. Employees who participate are granted an option to purchase company shares at the market value prevailing at the date of grant. As with all approved schemes, unless the shares are quoted on a national stock exchange, the market value must be agreed by the Inland Revenue in advance of each grant of options.

The scheme may provide that the exercise of options is permitted at any time after grant. Alternatively, exercise may be made subject to restrictions. Some typical restrictions are:

- to permit exercise only after three or more years;
- to permit exercise of options as to 20% on or after the first year and 20% on or after each successive year so that only after five years is the option capable of exercise in full;
- to make exercise conditional on the individual's performance or the company's performance (this is less common).

If the employee is to obtain favourable tax treatment upon exercise of his option, he must exercise it between the third and tenth anniversary of the date of grant and must not exercise it within three years of an earlier exercise upon which he enjoyed favourable tax treatment. In addition the exercise must be in accordance with the Scheme rules and the Scheme must remain approved at the date of exercise.

There is a statutory limit on the value of options which an employee may hold unexercised under an approved scheme. This is four times the employee's earnings subject to Pay-As-You-Earn or £100,000, whichever is the greater.

Following the enactment of the Finance Act 1987, in the event of a takeover and providing that the acquiring company agrees, it is possible for an employee to substitute options over the new company's shares for the options over the old company's shares. Provided that the qualifying conditions are met, the new options will qualify for favourable tax treatment on exercise.

An example of how a typical scheme might operate is set out below:

In September 1985 John Brown, a divisional director in H Robinson Engineering Limited was offered an option over the Company's 25p ordinary shares to the value of his current salary of £30,000. At the time the share price was 60p and he received an option over 50,000 shares.

Three years later, in September 1988, the share price has increased to 100p per share. He decides to exercise his option over all 50,000 shares and approaches his bank manager to borrow sufficient funds to meet the purchase price. The bank manager agrees to help provided he sells sufficient shares to repay the loan.

The scheme is an approved scheme and John is exercising his rights within the time scale laid down in the statute which ensures he will not pay income tax on the exercise of his options. His position will be as follows:

Value of shares (September 1988) 50,000 × 100p = £50,000
Cost of shares   50,000 × 60p = £30,000

Increase in value over 3 years = £20,000 with no income tax to pay.

John sells all his shares the same day for a net sum after brokerage charges of £49,200. Providing that he has not realised any other chargeable gains in the tax year he will pay capital gains tax calculated as follows:

	(£)
Sale proceeds	49,200
less price paid	30,000
	19,200
Less the annual exempt amount	6,600
	12,600
Capital gains tax payable = 12,600 × 30% =	3,780

NB No indexation allowance is due as John held the
   shares for 1 day only.

	(£)	(£)
Net profit to John =		19,200
less tax	3,780	
less bank loan charges, say	100	3,880
Total net gain =		15,320

In conclusion share options are an increasingly popular element in an executive's benefit package and are rapidly becoming the norm. Share options can form a useful 'golden handcuff' to encourage key personnel to stay with their employer and it is for this reason that schemes typically provide that options become capable of exercise or 'vest' only after the passage of some time. If shares perform particularly well, however, a scheme can in certain circumstances create an opposite effect, in that an executive can receive such a useful sum of money after exercising his options and selling his shares that he can retire early or set up his own business.

What types of company can operate an approved share scheme?

Most companies are able to do so, both those with some form of market quotation and wholly private companies. For any group of companies, quoted, unquoted or private, the shares in the parent company (whether UK or overseas) may be used. Unquoted shares in a subsidiary whose ultimate parent is quoted and not a close company may be used also.

Is it possible to use a special class of share capital in operating an approved share scheme?

It is possible to use a special class of share capital but the legislation which applies to approved share schemes is designed to ensure that employees receive a genuine stake in the equity of their employer. For this reason the shares used must be ordinary shares (not non-participating preference shares) which rank equally with other shares of the same class. They must be fully paid up, not redeemable and not subject to any restrictions which do not attach to all shares of the same class.

Where a company has more than one class of ordinary share capital the company must either be employee-controlled or the share capital must satisfy further complex conditions.

It is possible however to arrange matters so that for example non-voting ordinary shares are used or preference shares with dividends linked to profits.

How much of the company's equity can be set aside for a share scheme?

For a company which does not have (or does not wish to attract) institutional investors such as pension funds or insurance companies the percentage of equity available for a company share scheme will be at the discretion of the shareholders. However, where a company has institutional investors, the investment protection committees such as:

• The Association of British Insurers;

- The National Association of Pension Funds;
- The Association of Unit Trust Managers; and
- The Association of Investment Trust Companies

have issued guidelines on share schemes which need to be taken into account. The most important of these guidelines which concerns the percentage of equity set aside provides that no more than 10% of the ordinary share capital may be put under option or issued under all of a company's employee share schemes (whether approved or not) within any 10 year period. Other guidelines concern the conservation of benefits for future participants, restrictions on who may participate, the level of participation and the timing of the grant of options.

In July of 1987 the Association of British Insurers announced changes to their guidelines, the most radical of which was the requirement that options should be capable of exercise only if there has been real growth in the earnings per share over the 3 years following grant.

What are the main features of Profit Related Pay?

Under the profit related pay (PRP) provisions of the Finance (No 2) Act 1987, private sector employees who pay income tax through the Pay-As-You-Earn system (PAYE) (but not controlling directors) may have up to one half of PRP pay free of tax up to a maximum of £3,000 or 20% of pay whichever is the lower. Thus the maximum tax free pay is £1,500. National Insurance Contributions remain payable.

All types of businesses can operate PRP, whether companies, partnerships or sole traders. The scheme can apply to a group, a whole company, a whole business or an employment unit within a business or company. The principal feature of the scheme is that an employer will distribute PRP to employees from money set aside in a PRP Pool. There must be a clear link between the PRP Pool of the specified employment unit and its audited profits. This Pool can be calculated by reference to a simple proportion of profits or by reference to year on year changes in profits. The Pool can be calculated as frequently as desired but must be calculated at least once a year.

In order for PRP to be introduced into a business, the scheme must be registered with the Inland Revenue before the relevant profit year begins. The application for registration must be endorsed by an independent auditor's report and PRP must be paid and tax relief given to the employee through the PAYE system.

At least 80% of full time employees in the employment unit must participate in the scheme although new employees may be excluded for up to three years. A scheme must last at least one year and at the end of each PRP period an independent auditor's report must be lodged with the Inland Revenue confirming that the scheme and tax relief have been operated properly. If profits remain unchanged from their level prior to the introduction of the PRP scheme, at least 5% of the total pay of participating employees must be paid as PRP.

An example of how PRP might work for an individual employee is given below:

> Tom Pearce works for the Greymare Saddle and Harness Company Limited. His employer has set up a Profit Related Pay Scheme under which 15% of the company's annual profits have been set aside as a PRP Pool.
>
> The company profits amounted to £50,000 pre tax compared to the company's annual pay bill of £100,000.
>
> Tom Pearce earns £10,000 per annum and his entitlement under the scheme is calculated to be £1,000. The limit on which PRP can be tax relieved is £3,000 or 20% of *total* pay whichever is the lower, Tom Pearce is entitled to tax relief on up to £2,200 (20% of £11,000). Since Tom's PRP entitlement falls within the limits he will be relieved of tax on £500 of his pay (i.e. one half of £1,000).
>
> As Tom is chargeable to tax at the basic rate the saving of tax is worth £500 × 27% = £135 to him.
>
> Profit related pay is not relieved from National Insurance Contributions (NIC) and since Tom is paid less than the upper earnings limit for employee (NIC) purposes, he will pay additional NIC of £90 (9%) on the £1,000.

Are PRP schemes a good idea?

The view of the Government is that by introducing a variable element into employees' pay, an incentive will be provided to employees to take a more direct personal interest in the success of their business. Employers, for their part, when faced with adverse market conditions will be relieved of some of the pressure to shed jobs in order to cut costs (because the PRP element of earnings would be automatically reduced).

PRP, as with any form of cash bonus scheme, must be introduced with care and with proper regard to the cost given a variety of market conditions. Unless this is fully considered in advance, in extreme circumstances a company could find that it was obliged to pay out large bonus payments when the cash flow position of the business would not permit it.

It is important to note that once the PRP scheme has been established the PRP profit pool must be paid out in accordance with the scheme rules regardless of the company's circumstances at the time. Although an employee's share of the pool may vary by reference to his salary, length of service or seniority the legislation makes no provision for a ceiling to be placed on the amount which an individual receives. The 20% of pay or £3,000 limit refers only to that element of the PRP which qualifies for tax relief. The legislation does however permit a 'long stop' provision to be included in the scheme such that if profits increase by more than 160% compared to a specified base period, the excess of the profit over this limit may be disregarded when computing the PRP pool.

In conclusion, profit related pay should only be introduced after the full impact of the scheme on the company has been fully explored. In particular, draft profit and loss account figures should be produced for a variety of circumstances so that the sensitivity of the accounts to profit changes and the payment of PRP pay can be considered.

In order to obtain the benefit of improved employee motivation, care should be taken to explain the scheme fully to employees. Literature should be produced for further reference and for those employees who join the business later.

Employees should be informed of the profitability of the business and of business performance against budgets and targets. Opportunity should be given for questions to be answered perhaps by way of a regularly convened forum such as a workers council or employee association.

Finally the scheme itself should be subject to review from time to time to check that it is still meeting the needs of the business.

10
Personal Pension Schemes

How are state scheme pensions calculated?

The state pension can be made up of the following three main elements:

- The basic state pension; payment of this in full depends on the record of contributions over a working life.
- The state earnings-related pension ('SERPS') which is only paid to those who have paid Class I National Insurance contributions as employees since April 1978 on earnings between a lower and an upper earnings limit (band earnings). The self-employed cannot qualify for this element.

  Recent legislation (The Social Security Act 1986) will reduce the earnings related pension in the following respects:

  (i) Pensions are to be based on lifetime average earnings rather than on the best 20 years.
  (ii) The pension is to be 20% of band earnings rather than 25%.
  (iii) The pension that can be inherited by a spouse is one half rather than the full amount.

- The graduated state pension based on contributions paid between 1961 and 1975.

What are personal pensions?

The term 'personal pension' refers to arrangements under which an individual will have his own 'fund' and pension benefits will be provided to meet his own preferences. Under the Social Security Act 1986 personal pensions become available from 1 July 1988.

Retirement annuities are the original form of personal pension arrangements for the self-employed or employees not in pensionable employment. These will be replaced by personal pensions although existing contracts may be continued.

Who can have a personal pension?

The self-employed and employees not in a company pension scheme (unless it only provides death benefits).

From 6 April 1988 employers will not be able to enforce compulsory membership of their pension schemes unless it is non-contributory and provides death benefits only. Existing members of schemes will have the right to opt out and effect personal pensions from 1 July 1988, but the employer will not be obliged to contribute directly to a personal pension.

What are the tax rules for contributions to personal pensions?

Broadly speaking personal pensions will operate in the same manner as retirement annuities. There will be no limits on the pensions provided but the maximum direct contributions payable each year will be as follows:

Age previous 6 April	Percentage of net relevant earnings
50 or less	17.5
51–55	20.0
56–60	22.5
61–74	27.5

These contributions will be fully allowable for tax purposes and accumulate in a fund not subject to income or capital gains tax. The contributions payable by the DHSS to contracted-out personal pensions (see below) are in addition to the above figures.

An employer may contribute to a personal pension if he wishes, but the above overall limits must not be exceeded. Employees will not be allowed to have a personal pension and be a member of a company scheme unless the latter provides only death in service benefits.

Employees will pay premiums net of basic rate tax while the self-employed will continue to reclaim tax through their tax return as at present. There will be provision for carrying forward unused contribution allowances and relating back contributions, similar to those presently applicable to retirement annuities (but not for employer contributions).

Who can provide personal pensions?

Retirement annuity rules limited the provision of policies to insurance companies, but other types of providers can be used for personal pensions. These include banks, building societies and unit trusts. Investor protection legislation applies to personal pension contracts but there will not be any restriction on charges.

How will personal pensions relate to the state scheme?

An employed person who takes out a personal pension will be able to elect that it be contracted-out of SERPS. The employer and employee will pay national insurance contributions at the full contracted-in rate. After the end of each financial year the DHSS will pay an amount equal to the contracted-out rebate of 5.8% of band earnings for the previous financial year, plus an amount representing tax relief on the employee's part of the rebate to the chosen pension provider.

Certain contracted-out personal pensions will also be eligible for an additional 2% of band earnings, as an incentive to contract-out. The incentive can be available for the tax years 1987/88 to 1992/93. Employees who have been in contracted-out employment for at least two years, however, cannot claim the 2% incentive unless they leave the company pension scheme before 6 April 1988. (This date has yet to be confirmed at the time of going to press.)

Although individuals will not be limited to one personal pension scheme, the contracting-out rebate can only be placed in any tax year with one scheme.

What are the benefits from a personal pension?

The benefits which an individual can take are not limited like those for company schemes. The pension which will be secured will be determined by the value of the accumulated fund and annuity rates available at the time of retirement. An individual will be able to draw his benefits at any age between 50 and 75 and will be allowed considerable flexibility in the form of them. For example a personal pension, spouse's pension, increases in payment, or tax free cash will be allowed.

The retiring individual may exchange part of his pension for a tax-free cash sum up to the lower of 25% of the fund or £150,000 per contract. Under the existing retirement annuity arrangements the tax-free cash sum must not exceed 3 times the residual annuity subject again to £150,000 for contracts effected on or after 17 March 1987. For those wishing to maximise the tax-free cash sum it may be advantageous in certain cases to take out retirement annuity contracts prior to 1 July 1988.

The flexibility is restricted for contracted-out personal pensions. The contributions paid by the DHSS must be accumulated separately and applied at State retirement ages. They cannot be used to provide a lump sum. This part of the fund must be used to provide a personal pension normally continuing at half rate to a surviving spouse. Both pensions have to increase at 3% per annum or the RPI if less. Insurance companies must offer rates which are the same regardless of sex and marital status.

How do I choose a personal pension contract?

In choosing a personal pension contract the following should be considered:

- likely future investment performance;
- charges;
- subsequent transfer terms;
- flexibility.

Employees would then need to decide whether or not the personal pension should be contracted-out.

As an alternative to a personal pension, a 'free-standing' AVC (see page 109) may provide some of the attractions of a personal pension but without the loss of company scheme benefits.

Should I contract-out?

For younger employees who are not in a pension scheme, it should be worth taking out a contracted-out personal pension, even if only the rebate is invested. A younger employee should expect to receive greater benefits through his personal pension than he could receive from SERPS, depending on investment performance and other factors. For older employees it is unlikely to be financially advantageous to contract-out a personal pension. This is illustrated by Table 10.1 which shows the estimated cost of providing the Guaranteed Minimum Pension (GMP) expressed as a percentage of band earnings. The GMP is broadly the additional pension which would have been earned from the state scheme.

Table 10.1 *Average cost of GMP 1988–93 expressed as percentage of band earnings*

Age	Men	Women
16–19	2.2	2.9
20–24	2.2	3.0
25–29	2.4	3.5
30–34	2.8	4.2
35–39	3.4	5.2
40–44	4.3	6.6
45–49	5.4	8.7
50–54	7.1	10.9
55–59	9.0	12.5
60–64	10.5	—

(Main assumptions: 8½% investment return, 7% earnings inflation).

These rates should be compared with the effective DHSS contribution from contracting-out of 8.54% of band earnings (or 6.54% if the incentive is not available).

What is a loanback?

Building societies, banks and other lenders may accept an individual's projected tax-free cash sum at retirement as a means of repaying a loan such as a mortgage. Prior to retirement there are no capital repayments and interest only is paid. Some form of security for the loan such as property or shares, will normally be required since the pension fund itself cannot be used as security. Repayment of a loan using the proceeds of an individual's pension fund is tax efficient, but it should be realised that such arrangements involve loss of flexibility in that the borrower may have to take his pension benefits to pay off the loan at an unfavourable time. Most significantly, the use of the cash entitlement from the pension to pay off the loan reduces the total benefit available for retirement.

What about life assurance?

Under current retirement annuity rules, life assurance can be provided by a policy under Section 226A of the Taxes Act 1970. The limit of premiums payable for these policies is 5% of net relevant earnings, and the premiums are eligible for the full relief of tax at the highest rate paid by the individual. Contribution towards such policies must be deducted from the maximum amount available to contribute towards retirement annuity policies. Similarly under personal pensions individuals may contribute up to 5% out of the maximum to provide death benefits. These benefits should not normally be subject to inheritance tax.

11

Occupational Pension Schemes

What are the tax rules for employers' pension schemes?

Company pension schemes, that is pension schemes organised by employers for their employees, must be approved under the conditions of the Finance Act 1970 and must follow the rules there laid down if they are to obtain favourable tax treatment. On obtaining Inland Revenue approval a scheme is known as an 'exempt approved scheme' receiving the following tax relief:

- contributions by an employer are deductible in computing taxable profits;
- employees can get a tax deduction for their contributions up to 15% of their remuneration;
- income and capital gains of the pension fund are exempt from tax;
- life assurance cover can be arranged so that proceeds are exempt from tax;
- a tax-free lump sum can be paid at retirement.

Does this mean that employers' contributions to pension schemes are unrestricted?

Pension schemes approved by the Inland Revenue have a built-in restriction because the benefits must be within certain limits. The contributions payable must not exceed those necessary to provide the scheme benefits. Contributions are virtually unrestricted up to those limits. If the accumulated funds are in excess of those required to provide promised benefits, the trustees are required to follow defined procedures for reducing the surplus.

What are the benefits allowed?

These include the following:

- A pension at normal retirement age of up to two-thirds final salary.
- Part of the pension may be exchanged for a lump sum of up to one and a half times final salary. As from 17 March 1987, for all new schemes or new members of existing schemes, there is an additional limit on the amount that can be taken as a tax-free lump sum related to a maximum salary of £100,000.
- On death, a pension for the spouse of up to four-ninths of employee's final salary.
- A tax-free lump sum on death in service of up to four times salary.
- Pensions may be increased in line with the Retail Price Index during the course of payment.

There are a number of concessions which in special circumstances can increase these limits.

Why is a pension scheme for employees able to provide more generous benefits than a personal pension?

Owing to the cost, few employee pension schemes maintained by small businesses are funded to provide the maximum allowable benefits. For employers wishing to provide the maximum benefits, however, there is virtually no restriction on their contributions provided that the scheme can absorb further funding, although the Inland Revenue may insist on spreading the tax relief on an exceptional single contribution over several years. This contrasts with the personal pension rules where allowable contributions are normally limited (see page 100).

It is worth pointing out that membership of an employer's scheme providing death in service benefits only, does not preclude an employee or director from effecting personal pensions. The small businessman may well find that the personal pension contribution limit is adequate for what he can afford towards pension provision, and the relative simplicity of a personal pension makes that a preferable arrangement, with death in service benefits provided by an employer's scheme. Individual circumstances need to be considered.

What is meant by a final salary scheme?

A final salary scheme is one where the level of benefits is defined. The benefit formula is usually expressed as a fraction of final salary, where the definition of final salary can have a range of interpretations permitted by the Inland Revenue, stretching back to thirteen years prior to normal retirement date.

By basing retirement benefits on a final salary, such schemes are advantageous to members by providing an automatic hedge against inflation. However, the disadvantage from the employer's point of view is that there is an open-ended liability, and the cost, especially for smaller schemes, can vary substantially from year to year.

How does this differ from a money purchase scheme?

For money purchase schemes the contributions rather than benefits are defined. These schemes have advantages for the employer by protecting him against the open ended liability found with final salary schemes, and for the employee in that at any given time he knows exactly how much money is being set aside to provide him with benefits.

Money purchase schemes also provide a flexible approach to pension provision, as the accumulated fund at retirement may be used to provide benefits in accordance with a member's own preference at that time.

What is an individual pension arrangement (IPA)?

An IPA is a company pension scheme established specifically for one employee. Such schemes may be suitable to top up a senior executive's normal scheme entitlement so as to approach Inland Revenue maximum levels.

If confidentiality is desired, this can be safeguarded by providing such a top up through an IPA rather than through the main company scheme.

Can a company scheme contract-out?

If an employer operates a pension scheme which can meet certain requirements then he can apply to contract his employees out of the state earnings-related pension scheme

(SERPS). Both the employer and his employees then pay lower contributions to the State scheme. The contracted-out employer's pension scheme must provide the employees with at least a guaranteed minimum pension (GMP). This broadly matches the additional pension which they would have earned from the State scheme.

From 6 April 1988 money purchase schemes, subject to a minimum level of contributions, will be able to contract-out of SERPS without having to promise the GMP. As a special incentive between April 1988 and March 1993, an additional 2% of band earnings will be paid into such schemes by the DHSS for employments becoming contracted-out for the first time after 31 December 1985.

What are the merits of contracting-out?

For the smaller company the administrative and other complications involved in contracting-out in its original form did not usually make this option feasible. Money purchase contracting-out may well however be worth looking at. For the larger company the question of whether it would be financially advantageous to contract-out depends amongst other things on its membership structure and the decision may be marginal. Again a money purchase contracted-out scheme, possibly as an addition to an existing scheme, may be attractive.

Should I use an insured scheme or self-administered scheme?

Shareholder directors of family companies may be interested in either fully self-administered or a mixture of insured and self-administered ('hybrid') pension schemes. Under such schemes provision may be made for part of the funds to be invested in or lent back to the business at a commercial rate of interest. This can overcome, to some extent, the objection that pension fund monies are lost to the company once they are paid over, but at the expense of some risk to the security of the pension. A major advantage of this type of arrangement, apart from investment flexibility, is that it can offer better value for money than conventional insured arrangements. There are a large number of hybrid schemes available and professional advice is essential to evaluate the merits of each.

For employees of small companies, many insurance

companies offer simplified packages to establish and administer pension schemes. Such schemes are usually run on a money purchase basis.

For larger company pension schemes, employers should consider unitised funds run by insurance companies and other institutions, or fully self administered arrangements.

Are controlling directors subject to special rules for employers' pension schemes?

All directors, including shareholder directors, may also qualify for pension benefits under approved occupational pension schemes. Although there may be restrictions upon the pension entitlements of directors, these are not likely to have serious effects unless remuneration is increased substantially in the last two years of working life.

What are additional voluntary contributions (AVCs)?

AVCs are an employee's own pension contributions to a company scheme over and above the normal employee contribution rate. The maximum total employee contribution rate is 15% of remuneration. Therefore AVCs can be used to top up an employee's contribution rate to the maximum 15% providing this will not result in benefits in excess of the Inland Revenue maximum.

Two important changes were introduced in the Finance (No 2) Act 1987:

(i) Members will be able to establish their own free-standing AVC arrangement.
(ii) Members are free to vary the amount and timing of their AVCs, subject to the overall limit of 15% of remuneration.

One restriction imposed by the Act is that under any new AVC arrangement from 8 April 1987, it will not be possible to commute the proceeds into a tax-free lump sum.

It is expected that individual members of schemes will be able to use free-standing AVCs to contract-out of SERPs.

What is salary sacrifice?

Under these arrangements, an employee takes a reduction in his remuneration to enable the employer to make an equivalent increase in his pension contribution. This can be advantageous where an employee is already paying the maximum 15% contribution, but finds his expected retirement benefits still fall short of the Inland Revenue maximum.

However, there are drawbacks to salary sacrifice arrangements. Firstly, if it is part of the pensionable pay that has been sacrificed the pension benefits at retirement or on death may be affected. Secondly, there is the administrative inconvenience of amending the employee's contract of employment and notifying and providing written evidence to the Revenue, if the amount sacrificed exceeds £5,000 per annum. It is important to note that if remuneration already earned is sacrificed, it remains part of the employee's assessable earnings and subject to taxation. It is therefore vital that the precise arrangements for introducing a salary sacrifice agreement be handled carefully and professional advice should be sought.

What happens if I leave a company pension scheme?

Early leavers are currently required to have at least five year's scheme membership in order to have a statutory right to a preserved pension. From April 1988 this will be reduced to two years. The options on leaving for these employees are as follows:

 (i) The benefits may be left in 'deferred' form until normal retirement age subject to a degree of protection against inflation.
(ii) A transfer value may be paid to a new employer's pension scheme, an insurance company's 'buy-out' policy or a personal pension.

For those members not entitled to preserved benefits, they may be able to take a refund of their own contributions.

What is a buy-out policy?

Under the Social Security Act 1985, members leaving employers' pension schemes can effect an individual policy with an insurance company of their choice as an alternative to a transfer value to another employer's pension scheme or preserved benefits. Those leaving after 1 January 1986 have a statutory right to this option whereas those who left prior to that date must rely on scheme rules to determine whether a buy-out policy is allowed. Professional advice is normally advisable to assess the merits of these policies. It will involve assessing the likely benefits compared with those offered by the other options.

Is entry to a company pension scheme compulsory?

From April 1988 employers will not be able to enforce compulsory membership of their schemes. Existing members will have the right to opt out. Membership of schemes providing life assurance only, however, can remain compulsory.

Should an employee opt out of a company pension scheme and get a personal pension instead?

A key factor is the period of time an employee feels they may spend with their present employer. They will need to consider:

- what benefits the existing company scheme provides;
- the net cost of the company scheme to them;
- the likely benefits from a personal pension.

Employees will also need to consider any loss in pension, death and disability benefits provided from the company scheme, and whether and on what terms, the employer will allow them to rejoin the company scheme at a later date.

What about life assurance?

Life assurance arrangements under company pension schemes are a valuable and relatively inexpensive provision.

Up to four times salary can be paid in lump sum form to a beneficiary on the death of a member while in company service. Providing this is paid to a beneficiary at the trustee's discretion, the lump sum benefit is exempt from inheritance tax.

Group life assurance schemes are commonly insured and non-contributory for members. For larger groups considerable discounts can be obtained for the life assurance premium, while requirements for medical information before the insurers accept risk for the life assurance cover become less onerous.

For those wishing to opt out of a company pension scheme,

it should be noted that membership of the company's life assurance arrangement may be lost.

If I am in ill health can I retire early?

Most company pension schemes will have provision for members retiring early due to ill health. In cases of serious ill health, where life expectancy is impaired, it may be possible to commute pension benefits in full.

If a member is retiring early due to ill health, life assurance cover should be considered. A company's cover for life assurance will normally cease on a member's leaving service or retirement. However, it may be possible for a member to elect a 'continuation option' whereby the member maintains the life cover with the insurers of the life assurance scheme, on an individual basis. Under such options medical evidence will not be required if taken up within a specific time limit; however the premiums, being on an individual basis, could prove expensive.

What is key-man insurance?

This is life or permanent health insurance, taken out by a company on the life of a key employee, to cover against loss of profits in the event of his death or absence due to sickness. The loss in profits would include the costs of finding and training a successor and interim loss of business.

The tax treatment of premiums and benefits under key-man insurance is at the discretion of the local Inspector of Taxes and should be cleared with them.

What other employee benefit arrangements can be provided?

Company sponsored permanent health insurance (PHI) schemes are becoming more popular. Under such schemes regular income is paid by an insurer when an employee is unable to work due to illness or accident. The benefit will only be payable once the employee has been disabled for a specific period, known as the deferred period, which is commonly 13 or 26 weeks, and can continue until the normal retirement age.

Benefits can also include payment of pension contributions to maintain the claimant in the company's pension and life assurance scheme.

Providing the PHI scheme does not require employee contributions the premiums paid by the employer will be allowable as a business expense for Corporation Tax, and will not count as part of the employee's remuneration. Claim payments passed on to the employee will be subject to income tax. If a PHI scheme includes a significant proportion of controlling directors or shareholders, tax relief may not however be available.

How does a pension scheme fit into personal financial planning?

A pension scheme does not provide a full investment programme for an individual, although in most cases it will be an essential part of any individual's savings arrangements. The provision of a regular pension on retirement is not just a safeguard but enhances the individual's freedom to settle his or her personal capital, including any capital derived from selling his or her business on retirement. The benefits can include both life assurance and substantial lump sums payable tax-free on retirement. An approved pension scheme is by far the most tax-efficient method of saving.

Due to the complexity of pensions and the variety of options and contracts available, professional advice should be sought before deciding how best to fund for retirement.

These pages on the pensions scene are based on our understanding of the legislation published to date including the Finance (No. 2) Act 1987 and the Social Security Act 1986. Further changes and clarification are however expected.

12

Planning for the future with a company

I am seriously considering the future of my company – what are the main tax considerations?

These will depend on the decisions taken concerning not only the commercial future of the business but also the needs of the proprietor and his or her family. The choices will include the following:

- an outright sale of the company;
- a partial sale either by private placing or by flotation;
- planning to pass control of the company intact to the next generation of the family;
- splitting up the company into different constituent businesses in the hands of different members of the family or different shareholders.

In all cases it is important to seek professional advice at the earliest opportunity, particularly if it is the intention to preserve the business into the next generation.

If I sell the company, is there any way of avoiding capital gains tax?

If the shares are sold to another company which acquires at least 25% of the ordinary shares, any capital gains tax liability can be deferred by accepting either shares or loan stock in the purchasing company in consideration for the shares being sold. The tax is deferred until the new shares or stock are ultimately sold, otherwise any profit arising on the sale of the shares will be chargeable to capital gains tax at the rate of 30%, subject to the 'retirement relief' mentioned below. If part of the consideration is satisfied in shares and part in cash, then the capital gains tax liability is restricted to the chargeable gain attributable to the shares disposed of for cash; tax on the remainder of the gain can be deferred.

Is it sensible to take shares and/or loan stock in lieu of cash in these circumstances?

This is really an investment decision. If the shares being offered by the purchaser are an attractive investment and readily realisable should cash be required in the future, then there is every reason to defer the tax liability. However, if a spread of investments is required, it may be necessary to sell at least a part of the holding for cash.

What often happens is that the vendors of a private company take shares in the purchaser and then realise only sufficient shares each year to ensure that any chargeable gain is within the annual capital gains tax exemption limited (currently £6,600). If gifts of shares or stock are first made to different members of the family other than the donor's spouse, the donor and the recipient can elect to hold over the gain (see pages 118–119). Each recipient can then sell sufficient shares to utilise fully his own capital gains tax exemption limit. Given the right circumstances (see page 120) there will be no inheritance tax to pay.

Are there any other reliefs available to reduce the capital gains tax liability on a sale?

Retirement relief may be available for gains up to £125,000 where the shareholder is 60 years of age or retires early on grounds of ill heath. To be eligible for the relief the retiring shareholders must own 25% of the company's voting shares (or 5% owned by the retiring shareholder and more than 45% owned by members of his or her family). Shares owned by the trustees of certain family settlements may qualify for this purpose. The individual must also have been a full time working director of the company for at least one year. The relief is given in proportion to the length of the qualifying period as a full time working director, and increases from £12,500 after one year up to a maximum of £125,000 after 10 years or more.

The indexation allowance (see page 119) may also reduce significantly the amount of the chargeable gain on a sale of shares.

What is the situation on a partial sale or flotation?

The same rules outlined above will apply. The chargeable gain on the shares sold or released to the market will be liable to capital gains tax in the normal way.

I have heard about the unlisted securities market – could I realise a part of my shareholding in this way, and are there any other markets available?

The Unlisted Securities Market (USM) is a market for company securities, regulated by the stock exchange but designed for smaller and less mature companies unlikely to apply for a full 'listing'. Shares quoted on the USM are freely traded by the public, so that Companies Act requirements apply and the directors must also accept the stock exchange general undertaking to keep the public informed of the company's affairs. The main advantages over a full listing, when there is a requirement that at least 25% of the ordinary shares must be held by the public, are the somewhat lower costs of entry and the minimum requirement for only 10% of the ordinary shares to be held in this way. More than 500 companies have obtained a USM quotation since the market was founded in 1980, many of them being 'family' companies. A number of companies have moved to a full listing after having a USM quotation.

The USM is not the only market available to the smaller company; in addition, there are the Over-The- Counter (OTC) markets and the Third Market.

The OTC markets, which are not under the auspices of the Stock Exchange, originally provided a market on which established family-owned businesses could raise finance. More recently, smaller and new companies, even start-ups, have been attracted to it – especially those which have raised finance under the Business Expansion Scheme (see Chapter 5).

The rapid growth of the OTC markets led the Stock Exchange to establish in January 1987 a new third market to provide a more regulated market, within the ambit of the Stock Exchange, for companies previously attracted to the OTC. As with the OTC markets, quotations on the third market will not disqualify companies from raising finance under the Business Expansion scheme.

The requirement for entry to both the OTC and the third market are generally less stringent than those for the USM and in neither case is there a minimum limit imposed for the proportion of shares which must be publicly-owned.

If shareholders realise part of their existing shareholdings on any of the markets, capital gains tax will be payable on gains arising on the shares sold, although there may be scope for mitigating or deferring the liability through the use of foreign trusts (page 139).

Can I raise cash by arranging for my company to buy in some of my shares?

This will only be feasible in very limited circumstances (see below). However it may be worth considering if the company is a trading company and Inland Revenue clearance can be obtained. The company will need to be able to show that the transaction is designed to benefit its trade, as well as meeting a number of other conditions of approval, the most important of which is that after the transaction the seller of the shares (and his or her associates including close relatives) may not retain more than 30% of the company. Exceptionally, the condition that the transaction must benefit the company's trade does not apply if the proceeds are applied by the vendor in meeting an inheritance tax liability of his arising on a death which cannot otherwise be paid without hardship.

What kind of transaction will the Inland Revenue approve?

An Inland Revenue press release states that it will be prepared to consider circumstances in which a company buys in shares held by an unwilling shareholder where it is shown that the presence of that unwilling shareholder is damaging to the company's trade. They normally expect the retiring shareholder to give up his or her entire interest in the company. Some examples which the Inland Revenue give are:

- where the company buys in shares in order to resolve a board-room disagreement which has an adverse effect on the trade;
- where an outside shareholder who has provided equity finance wishes to withdraw his or her investment.

- where the proprietor of a company is retiring to make way for new management.
- where a shareholder has died and his personal representatives or beneficiaries do not wish to retain the shares.

An example of circumstances where these guidelines might apply are those in which the retiring shareholder (and his or her spouse) are disposing of their shares in the company for the benefit of their adult children who will carry on the business in the next generation. Moreover the circumstances in which a scheme for the company to buy in its own shares can be said to benefit its trade are not necessarily limited to these guidelines. Any reasonable case may be worth trying, provided that all the technical conditions can be complied with.

If Inland Revenue approval is obtained, the shareholder's profit (if any) on sale of the shares will be taxed as a capital gain. If clearance is not obtained the proceeds paid by the company, to the extent that they are not merely repayments of the original amounts subscribed for the shares, will be taxed as income in the same way as a dividend.

If I transfer shares by way of gift to members of my family in the next generation, will I have to pay capital gains tax?

A short answer to this question is 'not necessarily', because a transferor and transferee can elect jointly that no charge to capital gains tax will arise on the transfer.

A gift of shares is treated as a disposal at market value for capital gains tax purposes, and a liability can arise if the value of the shares exceeds their cost (as adjusted by the 'indexation allowance').

If a gift is made by one individual resident in the UK to another, a claim may be made for the gain to be 'held over'. This claim, which must be made by both the transferor and the recipient, means that the transferor does not become liable to capital gains tax on his or her notional gain, and the recipient is treated as acquiring the shares at their market value less the amount of the transferor's notional gain which has been held over. Tax will arise when the new owner sells the shares, and there are rules which trigger off the gain if the new owner becomes non-resident.

The relief is often referred to as 'holdover relief'. It is also available when gifts are made to trustees provided that the transferor and the trustees are resident in the UK. Trustees and beneficiaries may also make a claim, for example, in circumstances where trust assets are transferred to a beneficiary.

If the shares pass on death there is no capital gains tax charge, and the beneficiaries acquire the shares at their market value at the date of death and not at the original cost of the deceased. This is more beneficial for capital gains tax than adopting the holdover treatment mentioned above.

Whilst holdover relief can be used to defer payment of capital gains tax on the gift of interests in a family business during the lifetime of the proprietor, this treatment is not available on a commercial sale of shares. In such cases deferral of capital gains tax is only available under the 'paper for paper' rules (page 114), or exemption may be available through retirement relief.

What is meant by indexation of capital gains tax?

As from 1982 an individual (or company) has been able to add to his base cost in calculating capital gains tax an amount known as an indexation allowance. The allowance is intended to give relief from tax on inflationary gains.

The allowance is calculated by applying to the cost of the asset the percentage movement in the retail price index from the later of March 1982 or the date of acquisition. Allowance is not therefore given for inflation prior to March 1982 and in the case of assets held for a long time with a low cost the value of indexation allowance would appear limited. Nevertheless, for disposals after 5 April 1985 an election can be made to calculate the allowance by reference to the value of the asset at 31 March 1982 (provided the asset was acquired before that date) instead of cost. This may considerably increase the amount of the allowance.

There are special rules for the identification of shares where the taxpayer has bought shares of the same class at different times. Generally speaking, the taxpayer's shares are identified on a last in first out basis which, although resulting in the lowest indexation allowance, may produce the lowest overall gain if the value of the shares has increased over the period of accumulation of the shareholding. In circumstances where a particular shareholding has been acquired piecemeal over a long period of time the identification rules are complex and advice should be sought.

What are the inheritance tax consequences of making lifetime gifts of shares?

The inheritance tax (IHT) consequences will depend upon the identity of the recipient, the period which elapses between the date of the gift and the death of the transferor, and the extent to which the transferor retains any sort of interest in the gifted property:

- where the gift is between individuals no IHT is payable on the occasion of the gift;
- where the gift is by an individual in favour of the trustees of certain 'favoured' trusts, again no tax is payable when the gift is made;
- subject to the availability of exemptions, all gifts made within seven years of death are subject to IHT although there are provisions which taper the tax charge where the death occurs more than three years after the gift;
- whenever IHT is chargeable the tax is calculated by reference to the cumulative transfers made by the donor in the previous seven years;
- in order to make an effective gift for IHT purposes, the donor must relinquish all (or virtually all) benefit in the gifted property.

The rates of IHT applying to chargeable transfers on or after 17 March 1987 are:

Cumulative chargeable transfers (after exemptions and reliefs)

Lower limit (£)	Upper limit (£)	Rate (%)	Cumulative tax (£)
0	90,000	Nil	Nil
90,001	140,000	30	15,000
140,001	220,000	40	47,000
220,001	330,000	50	102,000
Over 330,000	—	60	—

IHT is charged on 'chargeable transfers'. These are transfers which are not covered by exemptions and which reduce the transferor's estate. The extent of this reduction does not necessarily correspond with the value of the gifted assets.

Does this mean I can now give away my shares without paying any tax?

Yes, the CGT holdover provisions coupled with the IHT rules exempting transfers to individuals and favoured trusts mean that you will avoid paying any tax on such gifts if you survive the transfer by at least seven years. The particular types of trust which qualify for the favoured IHT treatment are:

- 'interest in possession' trusts, where the beneficiaries are normally entitled to income for the rest of their lives or for some lesser stipulated period;
- 'accumulation and maintenance' trusts, created for the benefit of the younger generation – those under the age of 25;
- 'disabled trusts' for the benefit of persons either mentally or physically incapable of managing their own affairs.

From what you say, it seems that if I am to achieve any IHT savings by making lifetime transfers, I have got to cut myself off completely from the gifted property?

The position is not quite so straightforward. The legislation talks of the subject matter of the transfer being enjoyed 'virtually to the entire exclusion of the donor' so that exceptions will be made where the reservation of benefit is small.

An unfortunate feature of the legislation is that a transferor will be unable to obtain an advance ruling as to whether he has retained a benefit in any lifetime disposition. The position will not be known until his death, obviously too late to take any corrective action. The implications of being treated as having retained a benefit as at the date of death are:

- the property in which the benefit has been retained is deemed to be comprised in the estate at the date of death and taxed accordingly; and
- the presence of the property in the estate is likely to increase the overall rate of IHT payable on the death, thereby increasing the tax attributable to the rest of the deceased's property.

There are specific exceptions from the reservation of benefit rules relating to gifts of land or chattels where the donor pays a market rent for his continued occupation or enjoyment of the property.

There are no specific provisions relating to the reservation of benefit in gifted shares but it is thought that the following 'retained interests' do not offend the 'reservation of benefit' rules:

- Voting rights attaching to other personally owned shares in the same company.
- Voting rights attaching to trustee shareholdings.
- Remuneration and other benefits which constitute 'reasonable commercial arrangements'.

On the other hand, a transaction such as the creation of a discretionary trust by an individual who retains an interest therein as a discretionary object would quite clearly be caught. As a result, the settled property would still be treated as comprised in the settlor's estate on his eventual death. Unlike the income tax legislation, the IHT rules do not expressly preclude the reservation of a benefit by the transferor's spouse. This means that a settlement with a beneficial class including the donor's husband or wife may prove to be a suitable vehicle for the individual who does not wish to cut himself off completely from the gifted wealth. This is, however, subject to the proviso that where a benefit does arise to the spouse during the settlor's lifetime, it will be necessary to satisfy the authorities that the settlor has not indirectly benefited if the application of the rules is to be avoided.

What is the position if I make a gift, initially reserving myself a benefit, but then excluding myself at some later stage?

The initial gift will be ineffective for IHT purposes and the transfer will be deemed to have been made at the time of exclusion. You will then have to survive the exclusion by at least seven years to avoid a tax charge on your death.

Accepting that I can avoid reservation of benefit problems, what happens if I die within seven years of an effective gift?

Let us first consider gifts between individuals and gifts into the favoured type of trusts, all of which do not incur a tax charge at the time of gifting.

If death occurs within the ensuing three years, IHT becomes payable on the gift at the rates obtaining on the date of death. Because the tax is cumulative, the rate will depend upon the value of other transfers made by the donor in the seven years prior to the gift. The rate will be applied to the value transferred at the time of the gift subject to the availability of exemptions and reliefs. Subject to certain conditions, relief is available if the gifted property has fallen in value since the date of the original gift. Unless the donor specifies otherwise in his will, the tax will be payable by the donee.

The following is an example which assumes that an individual dies in 1995 having made a gift to a discretionary settlement of £40,000 cash in 1987 and £60,000 of quoted investments to his son in 1993. For the sake of simplicity, exemptions have been ignored and it has been assumed that rates of IHT have remained constant.

1987 Gift of £40,000 – no tax would have been payable at the time of the transfer since, although this was a chargeable transfer, it fell within the nil rate band of £90,000.

1993 Gift of £60,000 – no tax would have been payable at the time of the transfer since this was a gift between individuals.

1995 Death of transferor – no IHT would be payable on the 1987 gift since this was within the nil rate band and, in any event, was made more than seven years prior to death. IHT would, however, be payable by the son on the 1993 gift of £60,000, the rate of tax taking into account transfers made by the father within the seven year period prior to 1993, i.e. although the 1987 gift of £40,000 does not itself give rise to a liability, it does still feature in the tax calculation on the 1993 gift as follows:

IHT on £60,000 at rates referred to on page 63 applicable to transfers in excess of £40,000:

(£)		(£)
50,000	(the balance of the nil rateband)	–
10,000	at 30%	3,000
60,000	IHT payable by son	3,000

Tax is payable at the full rates on the 1993 gift since death occurred in the ensuing three years. As mentioned on page 120, had the death been more than three years after the gift, the rates of tax would have been tapered by 20%, 40%, 60% and 80% according to whether death occurred within year four, five, six or seven:

Death in year	% of full charge	Reduced tax charge (£)
4	80	2,400
5	60	1,800
6	40	1,200
7	20	600

In what circumstances can IHT become payable at the time a gift is made?

In broad terms, if you make a lifetime gift which:

- is not exempt;
- after taking into account reliefs, does not fall within the nil rate band;
- is not in favour of another individual or the trustees of one of the favoured trusts referred to on pages 137–139;

there will be some tax to pay on the occasion of the gift calculated by reference to your cumulative transfers in the previous seven years. The IHT will, initially, be charged at one half the usual rates but if you fail to survive the gift by seven years, there may be further tax to pay. In this event, the lifetime tax calculation will have to be reworked using the full rates obtaining at the date of death suitably tapered if this occurs in years four to seven. If the reworked tax exceeds the lifetime charge, the difference becomes payable by the donee. If it is less, there is no refund.

As in the case of other lifetime gifts, the tax is always arrived at on the basis of values at the time of the original transfer and not at the time of death.

The most common transfer which will give rise to a half rate charge is a gift into a discretionary trust.

I now understand how my donee can become liable for IHT if I do not survive the gift by seven years – could you explain how lifetime gifts affect the tax position on the rest of my estate which passes on my death?

Unless your estate qualifies for any exemptions (for example, the spouse or charitable exemptions) the whole of your wealth will attract a charge to IHT on your death at the rates referred to on page 120. Lifetime gifts which are themselves not exempt and which you have made within the seven years prior to your death will affect the rate of tax payable on your estate.

To summarise, depending upon an individual's pattern of lifetime giving, there may be three separate and distinct tax calculations to be made on his death.

- The tax payable on gifts within the previous seven years which did not suffer tax when made.
- The additional tax payable on gifts within the previous seven years which originally suffered tax at half the usual rates.
- The tax payable on assets remaining in the deceased's estate as at the date of his death.

Complications can arise where 'half-rate' gifts are preceded by 'free of tax' gifts in the seven year period, the explanation of which is beyond the scope of this book. It should be said, however, that in these circumstances, the donee of a 'half-rate' gift can, on the subsequent death of the donor, find himself saddled with an additional tax liability substantially higher than he may have expected.

What are the main exemptions from IHT?

The principal annual exemptions which are likely to be relevant to the owner of a family company are as follows:

- Transfers of up to £3,000 per annum are wholly exempt. This exemption is available to both spouses so that for husband

and wife the total figure is £6,000 per annum. The value of this exemption is doubled if business property relief (see below) is available at the highest rate.

- Transfers, regardless of the number made in any one year, are exempt if no single donee receives more than £250.
- Transfers between husband and wife are wholly exempt unless the transfer is made by a spouse who is domiciled in the United Kingdom to a spouse who is not. In this case, the exemption is limited to the first £55,000 of transfers.
- £5,000 can be given away free of tax by both husband and wife to each of their children in consideration of their marriage. The equivalent exemption for gifts by grandparents is £2,500 and for any other person £1,000.
- Regular transfers out of surplus income which do not affect the transferor's standard of living can be made free of tax.

These exemptions can be claimed against 'half-rate' gifts (those which are not tax free when made because, for instance, they are in favour of discretionary trustees) in order to reduce or eliminate the tax charge on the occasion of the gift or, in the case of gifts which were originally tax free, may be back-dated on the occasion of the death of the donor in the seven year period.

What are the main reliefs relating to companies?

The main relief is known as 'business property relief'. Provided certain conditions as to period of ownership are met, 50% of the value of the shares transferred by a shareholder with a majority holding in a trading company at the time of the transfer will be relieved from charge to IHT. This 50% relief also extends to 'substantial majority shareholdings' (defined as holdings of more than 25%) in unquoted trading companies. 'Unquoted' for this purpose means not quoted on a recognised stock exchange or dealt in on the USM.

The rate relating to transfers made by smaller minority shareholders in unquoted companies is 30%. There is also a 30% relief applying to transfers of certain assets used by a company which the transferor controls.

Shares in an investment company will not qualify for business property relief unless it is acting merely as a holding company for trading subsidiaries.

The main conditions referred to above, which must be satisfied if full relief is to be obtained, require at least two year's ownership by the transferor and:

- retention of the shares or assets by the transferee throughout the period between the date of the gift and the death of the transferor in the ensuing seven years, with the gifted property retaining its nature as qualifying business property throughout; or
- where the transferee has sold the property the reinvestment by him of the total sale proceeds in replacement qualifying property within 12 months of the sale.

It should be noted that shares in a company are not the only category of assets which constitute qualifying business property. The conditions can be satisfied where, for example, the proceeds of sale of gifted shares are 'reinvested' in the business of a sole trader or an interest in a partnership.

An example of a gift of business property which would not qualify for the relief might be a gift of shares in an unquoted company subsequently acquired by a quoted company in a 'paper for paper' transaction during the period between the gift and the donor's death in the following seven years. The quoted shares would not normally constitute 'business property' in the hands of the donee at the time of the donor's death and IHT would be calculated without the benefit of business property relief.

What are the implications of failing to satisfy the retention or replacement tests during the seven years after a gift?

It depends whether the gift was chargeable at the time it was made.

If it was, business relief will have been granted at the time of the gift and reflected in the tax charged at half-rates. If for example, the transferor dies within the ensuing seven years and in the meantime the transferee has sold and not replaced the business property, relief will not be available when calculating the additional tax liability.

If, however, the original gift did not attract a tax charge initially (for instance, because it was a gift between individuals) the entire tax liability attributable to the gift will fail to attract relief.

Is it possible to pay the inheritance tax liability by instalments?

Yes, provided certain conditions are satisfied, the tax can be paid by equal annual instalments over ten years. The option to pay the tax in this way can apply where the gift is made on death or where, in the case of a lifetime gift, the transferee bears the tax liability. (This will normally be the case, for example, where the donor fails to survive the gift by seven years and the tax/additional tax becomes payable by the donee.)

The instalment option is not available unless the subject matter of the gift is 'qualifying property' which for this purpose comprises land, controlling shareholdings and, subject to certain conditions, unquoted minority shareholdings in trading companies. The conditions in question, which vary according to whether the property is gifted during lifetime or on death, relate to the value of the holding and its size in relation to the company's issued share capital. For example, a lifetime gift of a minority holding of unquoted shares will not qualify for the instalment option unless the gifted shares represent 10% or more of the company's issued share capital. Having said this, even if the conditions cannot be satisfied, the benefits of the instalment option can be obtained in circumstances where it can be proved to the satisfaction of the authorities that to pay the tax in one lump sum would cause undue hardship.

In addition, where a lifetime gift is involved, there are stipulations similar to the business relief conditions referred to on pages 126–127, that the gifted property (or its replacement) must retain its nature as qualifying property throughout the period up to the donor's or, if earlier, the donee's death.

Provided the instalments are paid on time, the tax liability on all categories of qualifying property, with the exception of nonagricultural land, does not attract an interest charge. With interest currently at the rate of 6%, the interest free facility represents a 'saving' to the taxpayer equivalent to about 27% of the inheritance tax liability. This is quite apart from the obvious cash flow advantage of being able to spread payment over ten years. In many cases, it will be possible to fund the annual tax charges out of dividend income on the gifted shares.

This valuable facility to pay tax by instalments, whether interest free or not, is understandably withdrawn where the gifted property is sold at any time during the ten year period; on that occasion, any unpaid tax becomes payable forthwith.

How does control of a company affect my liability to IHT?

A gift out of a controlling shareholding in a company will be eligible for the higher 50% rate of business property relief, as explained above. However, value attaches to control of a company and a majority shareholding (that is, one comprising more than 50% of the voting shares) will often have a substantially higher market value per share than a minority holding.

Can you explain this more fully?

The valuation of unquoted and unlisted shares (and in certain cases quoted shares as well) is related to the influence that the holding gives the owner over the affairs of the company. A shareholder who controls more than half the voting shares has control over the earnings and distributions of the company. The valuation of his holding will be made by reference to, or by taking account of, the full earnings of the company, and possibly by reference to the underlying value of the company's assets.

If the holding does not give the owner control, or any degree of influence, it is likely to be valued on the basis of the dividends which can reasonably be expected (or in some cases hoped for) in the future. Most companies pay dividends which are a fraction of earnings and many private companies pay no dividends at all. Valuations of a minority holding in a private company on a dividend yield basis will come to a different, and generally much lower, value per share than valuations on a full earnings basis.

Does this mean that a gift of shares which allows control to pass will be expensive in terms of IHT?

It could be, although, of course, only if you fail to survive the gift by seven years, or if the gift is not to another individual or a favoured trust. As mentioned on page 120, IHT is payable on the amount by which the transferor's estate is reduced by making the gift, and a gift which results in the donor's losing control of the company can reduce the value of his estate by more than the gifted shares valued in isolation.

How is this calculated?

If, for example, an individual holds 51% of a company and gives away a 2% holding, the amount of the reduction in that individual's estate will be equal to the difference between:

- a 51% shareholding valued on say a full earnings basis; and
- a 49% shareholding valued say by reference to expected dividend yield.

The difference between these valuations is likely to be a much larger figure than the value to the recipient of a 2% holding, unless the recipient personally obtains control.

Can tax on this value attributed to control be alleviated?

To some extent, yes. If you consider there is a real possibility that you might not survive the seven year period, it may pay to lose control by transferring a large block of shares to maximise the benefit from the higher (50%) rate of business property relief. If, on the other hand, there will be tax to pay on the occasion of the gift (if for instance you want to put your shares into a discretionary trust) and you think you stand a good chance of living a further seven years you might do better first to surrender control by transferring a small number of shares to another individual (tax free if you survive seven years) and follow this with a transfer of all or part of what will then be your minority interest into the discretionary trust. This is really a question of valuation.

Could I not lose control by transferring shares to my spouse?

On the face of it, this would achieve nothing for IHT purposes since, under what is known as the 'related property rule', shares owned by husband and wife have to be valued for the purposes of this tax on the basis that they form a single holding. Where joint control exists, a gift of shares by either husband or wife will be valued on the basis of a controlling interest.

However, some scope for planning may exist where there is a marked difference in the life expectancy of the spouses. In these circumstances, there is everything to be said for the transfer effecting loss of control to be made by the spouse with the potentially greater longevity in the expectation that survival for a further seven years will result in the avoidance of any IHT liability.

In instances where the younger spouse possesses no shares or insufficient shares there may be a case for an inter-spouse transfer (tax free under the spouse exemption) to enable the donee subsequently to effect the loss of control. Note, however, that to avoid the loss of business property relief in the event of the donee spouse's failing to survive his or her gift by seven years, the second gift should take place not less than two years after the first.

Do the same principles apply for quoted as for unquoted shares?

The valuation of quoted shares will depend on the quoted price although there will often be a premium ascribed to a controlling interest.

Business property relief at the rate of 50% may be attributed to a controlling interest in a listed company or one quoted on the USM but no relief is given for a minority interest.

Shares dealt in on the third market or the OTC markets are not treated as quoted for IHT purposes. The quoted price will provide an indication of value (with some premium for control), but for such shares business property relief may be available both for a controlling or substantial minority interest (at 50%) and a smaller minority interest (30%).

I now understand the implications of transferring shares to others, but what is the position regarding business assets which are in my ownership?

The capital gains tax and inheritance tax principles relating to the transfer of shares apply equally to gifts of assets which you own personally but which are used in the company's business, with the result that such gifts can be made without giving rise to an immediate tax liability.

In the event of an inheritance tax liability arising, however, the maximum rate of business property relief which can apply is 30% and only then if the following additional conditions can be satisfied:

- the asset in question must be a building, land, machinery or plant which immediately before the gift is used wholly or mainly for the company's business (this condition may not be satisfied where the transferor or any persons have personal use of the asset);
- the transferor must have a controlling interest in the company;
- shares in the company must themselves constitute qualifying business property.

The opportunity to pay the inheritance tax liability by instalments does not apply in the case of assets which are in your personal ownership but which are used in the company's business unless the assets consist of land, or buildings. In the case of agricultural land, if paid on time, the instalments will not attract interest.

If I wish to keep the business in the family, what should I be doing now?

You would be well advised to:

- take stock of your overall financial position in the light of current values;
- assess the likely requirements of yourself and your family taking into account the terms of your will and the potential IHT liabilities which may arise on your death and/or that of your spouse;
- consider whether and to what extent you are willing to divest yourself of any part of your wealth with a view to achieving tax savings;
- look at possible methods of achieving your aims.

Having gone through the steps referred to above, you may reach the conclusion that the potential IHT liabilities are either small enough to be disregarded or manageable insofar as your business interests are concerned (in that your heirs will be able to spread payment of the liability on such assets by instalments over 10 years). Alternatively, if you have left your entire estate to your spouse under your will you may feel that deferral of all

IHT liabilities until the death of the survivor achieves your principal aim of protecting the survivor's position.

If, however, you decide to do something about the potential liabilities this will inevitably mean that you will have to divest yourself of wealth during your lifetime.

Can you give me some broad guidelines to consider when passing on my business interests?

There is considerable incentive to divest yourself of property now rather than later, principally because the beneficial IHT rules permitting tax-free gifts to individuals and the favoured trusts (provided the donor survives at least seven years) are unlikely to survive any future change in government. Add to this the desirability of ensuring that the seven year period starts to run at the earliest possible opportunity and the case for acting without delay becomes even more convincing.

As a general principle, transfers of wealth should be made in favour of the younger rather than the older generation and since IHT is basically a 'once a generation' tax, if possible, the opportunity should be taken to skip a generation by making transfer to or for the benefit of grandchildren or even remoter issue.

Since, as mentioned on pages 123 and 125 IHT is always payable by reference to the value of the gifted property at the date of its transfer, lifetime giving (so long as no benefit is retained by the donor) has the effect of 'freezing' the value of the gifted property with the result that any future appreciation in its value is enjoyed by the donee completely free of IHT. It follows that it is always preferable to give away property which is expected to appreciate in value.

For example, gifts of shares at a time when a company is in a period of low profitability, rather than when profits are rising, would satisfy this criterion. In addition, if a new trading activity is planned by an existing company, the creation of a new company to undertake it in which the next generation can take an interest from the start may, if the activity is successful, have substantial tax-saving benefits.

The opportunity should be taken to use the annual exemptions on a regular basis since it should be remembered that gifts covered by the exemptions will not attract a tax charge even if the transferor dies within the ensuing seven years. Similarly, when making lifetime transfers, full advantage should be taken of the available reliefs, particularly business relief, if it is reasonable to assume that the qualifying conditions will continue to be met for at least seven years.

Whilst it is not strictly an exemption, the nil rate band of IHT (currently £90,000 or effectively £180,000 if 50% business property relief is available, pages 126–127) can be viewed as such bearing in mind that cumulative transfers within this limit are both tax free when made and, furthermore, drop out of the cumulative total of the transferor after seven years have elapsed. Substantial savings can therefore be achieved by making chargeable transfers of £90,000 every seven years.

Finally, the benefits which can accrue following an equalisation of estates between husband and wife should not be overlooked. Not only does it permit each spouse to utilise his or her reliefs and annual exemptions, but also the advantages outlined on pages 130–131, where life expectations differ significantly can be beneficial.

Are there many pitfalls of which I should be aware?

There are many traps into which the unwary may fall. The following list is by no means exhaustive.

- Beware of overstretching yourself when making lifetime gifts and always retain sufficient assets to support yourself and your dependants throughout the rest of your days.
- Bear in mind that the order in which gifts are made can affect the IHT liability of the donee should you be unfortunate enough to die within the seven year period.
- Where appropriate, warn the donee of any gift that your death within the seven year period will result in his having to meet a further tax bill.
- When giving property qualifying for business property relief warn the donee of the dangers of losing both the benefit of the relief and the option to pay the tax by annual instalments.
- If you are considering gifting assets currently showing significant capital gains, remember that an election for CGT holdover relief (page 32) does not eliminate the tax charge but merely defers it until the asset is subsequently disposed of by the donee. On the other hand retention of the asset until death wipes the capital gains tax slate clean.

- Ensure that for IHT purposes, you do not fall foul of the retention of benefit rules – if you do, you will not achieve any tax saving.
- If you are attracted to the possibility of saving IHT by, for example, channelling funds through your spouse (pages 131–134) do not overlook the associated operations provisions which may result in your intentions being frustrated. There should never be a binding requirement on the donee spouse to gift on the property and, generally speaking it is advisable to leave a reasonable interval between the original and any subsequent gifts.

To minimise the risk of falling into these traps, always seek professional advice.

What part can life assurance play in planning for inheritance tax on my business?

There are principally two areas where life assurance can help:

- in making provision for any IHT which will become payable on a gift on the death of the donor in the seven year period;
- in providing one's heirs with a tax-free sum with which to pay the IHT ultimately arising on death, whenever this occurs.

Where the requirement is to provide the IHT (or additional IHT) on a gift on the occasion of the donor's death within the seven year period it would normally be appropriate to effect seven year term insurance cover on a reducing basis to accord with the taper relief referred to on page 124. For the reasons stated on page 125, calculation of the required cover may not be entirely straightforward where there have been earlier gifts which were free of tax when made. In addition, where shares are gifted at a time when, for example, a USM flotation is envisaged during the ensuing seven years, there may well be a case for insuring on the basis that business property relief will not be available. The policy should always be written in trust for the donee in whose hands the proceeds could be tax free.

Insuring to cover the donee's potential IHT liability on gifted shares is not necessarily the complete answer since this does nothing to assist the beneficiaries of the remainder of the trans-feror's estate who, if death occurs in the seven year period, will effectively bear tax at the transferor's highest marginal rates. This results from the fact that the gift, which absorbs the donor's lowest IHT rates, will not drop out of the aggregation calculations until seven years have expired. In these circumstances, it may be advisable for the transferor to effect an appropriate amount of level term cover over the seven year period, the policy being written in trust for the heirs under his will.

Where the need is to provide a 'sinking fund' for the IHT ultimately payable on the deceased's assets at the date of this death, a whole life policy is appropriate:

- Once the policy is in force, the basic sum assured is guaranteed.
- The investment buildup is tax-efficient since insurance company funds enjoy beneficial rates of tax.
- If the tax liability will not arise until the death of the survivor of the husband and wife (because the survivor inherits all under the will of the first to die), a joint life and survivor policy will ensure that the funds are available when needed. The level of premiums on such policies takes account of the age of the younger spouse.
- If the policy is written in trust for the benefit of the younger generation (or, alternatively, if a member of the younger generation or trustees for them effects the policy on the life of a parent) the policy proceeds themselves can be received free of IHT on the life assured's death.

Other points relating to the use of life policies are as follows:

- Depending on the age of the life to be assured, a with-profits policy will usually be appropriate because the bonus additions will assist in providing for any increasing tax liability as the business itself expands.
- Where a policy is written in trust for the younger generation, the annual premiums will be regarded as annual gifts in their favour by the person paying them. These will not, however, generate a charge to IHT if they fall within the annual £3,000 exemption or, alternatively, the surplus income exemption.
- The premiums on policies effected by the younger generation on a parent's life may be financed by, for example, increasing the level of salary they draw from the business or distributing profits to them by way of dividend.

- Trustees can, if the trust deed permits, use income to meet premiums due on policies on the settlor's life.

Could a company pension scheme help in reducing IHT on my business?

A company pension scheme for directors, particularly a small self-administered scheme (see chapter 11) can be very useful in reducing the impact of IHT on a family company. This is because:

- both the assets and profitability of the company will be reduced by substantial transfers of funds into a pension scheme thus reducing the value of the company shares;
- death in service life assurance cover (written in trust for the younger generation) can be taken out on the lives of the older directors via the pension scheme and corporation tax relief thereby obtained on the premiums paid;
- the tax-free lump sum available at retirement can provide liquidity to fund lifetime gifts (to utilize available exemptions).

Might trusts have a part to play in IHT planning for my business?

Trusts can play an important part in tax planning for the family business. For example, by transferring shares in the family company to trustees it is possible to limit or even reduce the potential IHT liability attaching to them if they continue to be held directly by members of the family. By appointing himself one of the trustees, the transferor can retain some control over the shares, normally without falling foul of the reservation of benefit rules.

There are many different types of trust and advice will be needed to determine not only which is the most appropriate in the circumstances but also to assess the tax and related costs of creating it and the potential tax savings.

Three types of trust which might be worth considering are:

- discretionary trusts – the shares in the family company being held, at the discretion of the trustees, for the future benefit of members of the family;

- accumulation and maintenance trusts – to hold shares for the younger generation of the family (individuals under 25);
- interest in possession (or fixed interest) trusts where the entitlement of the beneficiaries is usually restricted to income only for the rest of their lives, the trustees having a discretion to advance capital to them.

Although a gift into a discretionary trust may give rise to an IHT liability and the trustees are themselves liable to IHT (and capital gains tax), the rules are currently such that the IHT burden is likely to be lower than it would be were the shares to remain in family ownership. One benefit of a discretionary trust arises from the fact that the death of a family beneficiary is not an event which will trigger any IHT charge. Another benefit is the facility to postpone any immediate decision as to who ultimately inherits the shares.

As mentioned on pages 121–122, any IHT benefits will be lost if the transferor includes himself as a beneficiary of a discretionary trust.

Provided they are drawn up in certain defined terms, accumulation and maintenance trusts for the benefit of younger members of the family receive beneficial treatment. For example:

- no IHT arises on the creation of the trust provided the settlor survives seven years;
- any future increase in value in the shares transferred to the trustees for the benefit of the younger generation on their attaining full age will be free of IHT;
- Dividends on the shares being accumulated by the trustees will suffer income tax at a maximum rate of 45%. The funds represented by income accumulations might themselves be used to good effect, for example, by the trustees acquiring further shares from the older generation or alternatively by the trustees taking out life assurance on the settlor's life.

The third type of trust – the 'fixed interest' trust – may have a use if for example there is a need to protect the beneficiary by tying up the capital. For IHT purposes, this type of trust (in common with the accumulation and maintenance trust) has the advantage that no IHT arises on its creation provided the settlor survives seven years. Furthermore, assets can be removed from such a trust tax-free, provided the beneficiary survives the removal by seven years.

Discretionary trusts created under wills can offer considerable flexibility to the deceased shareholder's executors and family to deal with the deceased's interest in the family company in the most tax efficient way. All trusts and particularly discretionary will trusts must be carefully drafted if IHT and other problems are to be avoided in the future. Professional advice is always necessary.

Can I avoid capital gains tax by placing my shares in an overseas trust?

Trusts which are established and administered overseas by foreign trustees and under which the transferor reserves himself an interest can have a significant role to play in deferring, and in some cases avoiding, capital gains tax on the sale of company shares or for example on a flotation on the USM. Normally there will be a capital gains tax charge on gifting the shares to the overseas trustees since holdover relief (page 118) cannot be claimed on transfers to non-residents but, once the shares are held in trust, tax on any future capital gains can be deferred by leaving the sale proceeds offshore in the hands of the trustees. The tax charge does not crystallise until the proceeds are paid to beneficiaries who are resident and domiciled in the UK.

It follows that maximum benefit can be obtained from these arrangements if shares which are expected to show substantial future growth are 'exported' at a time when their value is low, thus minimising the capital gains tax actually payable. Even this charge can be deferred by first appointing UK trustees who retire in favour of foreign trustees only when the sale/flotation is imminent.

Timing is crucial and there are many pitfalls in the arrangements.

The use of an overseas trust coupled with a foreign holding company can result in considerable tax advantages for shareholders who are not domiciled in the UK; effectively, their shares can be removed from the scope of both capital gains tax and IHT. Great care must, however, be exercised in implementing the arrangements and professional advice is essential.

If my children are already shareholders, can I allocate a part of the business to them and retain another part myself without tax penalty?

Breaking up an existing business into two or more separate businesses is not a simple operation and will always involve incurring substantial professional costs. It may be possible to create two or more companies to acquire separate trades, their shares then being exchanged for shares in the existing company. A reorganisation on these lines might be possible without creating an unacceptable tax liability either by liquidating the existing company or under the 'demerger' provisions of the tax legislation.

How important is it to my business to have a will?

If an individual does not leave a will, his property, including his business interests, will pass to the heirs in accordance with the rules relating to intestate estates. These rules may result in a wholly unsatisfactory situation developing after the person's death.

It is possible for the executors and the adult beneficiaries to agree to vary the terms of an unsatisfactory will but to avoid IHT penalties any such variation has to take place within two years of the death. This facility can be used if the will creates problems for the survivors in ensuring the continuity of the family company. This can, however, be a complex matter and is best avoided by having a well-drawn will and reviewing it periodically.

Executors can be given wide discretionary powers under the will. These afford them the flexibility to take appropriate action concerning the estate and the family business in the light of the situation arising as a result of the death and the wishes of the survivors.

What is the most important factor in tax planning for the future of my company?

Simply, start as soon as possible. Problems usually arise only in circumstances where planning is left until the last moment.

If the members of the older generation start to transfer their interests in the family business whilst they are comparatively young and before the full potential of the business is realised, the ultimate saving in IHT will be that much greater. A programme of lifetime transfers might be supplemented by the use of life assurance. If proper provision is made for retirement pensions it may be much easier to release capital to the next generation.

Lastly, this is a complex topic. The comments set out in this chapter of the book have touched only briefly on the problems and solutions to them.

13

Planning for the Future by the Sole Trader or Partner

As a sole trader or a partner in a firm, can I plan for the future in exactly the same way as if I were a shareholder in a company?

Not exactly. If you are considering the outright sale of the business as a going concern, you can do so without capital gains tax consequences if the sale is to a company in exchange for shares. Provided all the business assets other than cash are transferred to the acquiring company, the tax can be deferred until the new shares are ultimately sold. Retirement relief may also be available within the limits specified on page 34 in addition to which indexation relief (page 119) may operate to relieve inflationary gains.

If you wish to consider a partial sale of the business on the open market, either by placing or by flotation, for example on the USM or the third market, a first step will be to incorporate (with the relativley minor tax consequences referred to on pages 32–33) and, once the new company has established an appropriate track record, as a second step the desired flotation route can be considered.

How do I go about gifting my business or a part of it?

Because of the nature of the assets involved, gifting the business interests of sole traders and partners (particularly where it is desired to effect a wide spread of ownership amongst members of a family) is less easily accomplished than the gifting of shares in a family company. However, incorporation is not necessarily the answer for the sole trader, who has the option of going into partnership with his intended donees, or the partner, who is able to introduce new partners to his existing business. Where it is not desired to bring others into the business itself, there may be scope for gifting assets which are owned by the transferor but which are used in the business.

Can I make these gifts without paying any tax?

Yes, the capital gains tax holdover relief (pages 118–119) and the IHT treatment relating to gifts to individuals and favoured trusts (pages 137–139) apply to gifts of interests in businesses and business assets in the same way as they apply to transfers of shares.

In fact, there will be no need to elect for holdover treatment where, for example, in the case of a partnership a new partner is brought in on terms which constitute a bona fide commercial arrangement. In these circumstances, the disposing partner is treated as making a disposal for a consideration equal to his capital gains tax cost so that no chargeable gain (or allowable loss) arises. Normally, where a gift is involved the transferee will be a younger member of the transferor's family or another connected person and, in order to satisfy the 'bona fide commercial arrangement' criterion, it will be necessary to show that the incoming partner is being introduced on terms similar to those which would apply to an outsider. If it can be demonstrated that the new partner is relieving the transferor of a significant level of his partnership responsibilities, the commercial argument is likely to succeed.

In appropriate circumstances, commerciality coupled with a lack of donative interest on the part of the transferor partner can also result in the transfer of a partnership interest being outside the scope of IHT.

If IHT becomes payable by either myself or the donee, are there any reliefs available to reduce the liability?

Business property relief (pages 126–127) is available to sole traders and partners at either the 50% or 30% rates.

Subject to certain ownership and use conditions, 50% relief

applies to a transfer of an interest in his business (as opposed to business assets) by both a sole trader and a partner. It is possible for any liability on gifts of such interests to be paid by interest-free instalments as described on page 128.

Thirty per cent relief applies to gifts of land or buildings, plant or machinery used wholly or mainly in a partnership business, although similar relief is not available to a sole trader. The tax on gifts of land and buildings may be paid by instalments in the appropriate circumstances, without interest in the case of agricultural property.

It seems to me that if, having gifted part of the business, I remain a partner, the gifts with reservation provisions will apply – is that right?

Generally speaking, no. The mere fact that the donor of an interest in a business remains a partner is not considered sufficient to invoke the gifts with reservation rules.

Take the case of a father who is a sole trader and who takes his son into partnership by transferring to him an interest in the business. Thereafter, they share profits and losses in proportions which take account of their respective interests in the partnership assets and also reflect their respective expertise and involvement in the business (i.e. these are commercial arrangements which one would expect to see in a partnership between unrelated individuals). In these circumstances, it is not considered that the gifts with reservation rules will apply.

Consider also the case of an individual who owns agricultural land, who gifts a one-third share in the land to each of his two sons and who subsequently farms it in partnership with the donees. If profits and losses are shared equally and all three partners have a similar level of involvement in the farming operations, again the transferor is unlikely to be deemed to have retained a benefit.

Equality in sharing profits and losses does not necessarily mean that the mischief of the legislation will be avoided. For instance if, in the first example, the gift by the transferor is on the occasion of his retirement from farming and thereafter he has no active involvement in the partnership, his retention of a one-third interest in the business and its profits will almost certainly mean that his gift is ineffective for IHT purposes.

Can trustees be introduced as partners?

Yes. In fact, trustees may be the ideal recipients for gifts of business interests particularly where the beneficiaries are minors, or under the age of 25, or individuals whom the transferor does not wish to have a direct involvement in the trading activities.

Gifts can be made either into existing family trusts or new trusts might be created specifically to hold the gifted business interests. In either case, the trustees would have to be specifically empowered by the trust deed to engage in trading activities.

The most common types of trust all of which, depending on the circumstances, may be appropriate recipients for gifted business interests are briefly described on pages 137–139.

From an income tax point of view, trusts (such as accumulation and maintenance and discretionary trusts) which permit the accumulation of income in the hands of the trustees can be attractive; the maximum rate of tax suffered by trustees on income accumulations is 45% as against the maximum rate of 60% applicable to individual partners and sole traders.

What happens to my business when I die?

If you are a sole trader and intend to remain so and envisage that your business will be disposed of immediately after your death, it is not essential that your will should contain any specific provisions relating to the business; the reason for this is that your executors (or your administrators should you happen to die intestate) are empowered by statute to continue the business until it is broken up or sold as a going concern.

If, however, you wish the business to be continued after your death for the benefit of your heirs, you will need to give careful consideration to the terms of your will. An outright specific gift to your intended heirs is the simplest option. Alternatively, if you wish the business to be held in trust for, say, your surviving spouse or minor beneficiaries, you will need to appoint suitable trustees willing and able to accept the considerable responsibility of carrying on the business for the benefit of your heirs. Careful drafting will be required to ensure that the trustees have sufficient power to enable them to discharge their responsibilities and to ensure that they are suitably indemnified against losses. Professional advice must be taken.

If you are in partnership, it is likely that the partnership deed will dictate the way in which your interest in the business is to devolve upon your death. In this event, you will not be able to override the terms of the partnership deed by directing otherwise in your will. If, on the other hand, there is no bar to your executors (or, in the longer term, your will trustees), assuming your partnership responsibilities, you will need to incorporate in your will the powers and indemnities referred to above.

Index